BIG
KNITS

BIG

BOLD BEAUTIFUL DESIGNER KNITWEAR

KNITS

DAWN FRENCH
AND SYLVIE SOUDAN

CENTURY
London Sydney Auckland Johannesburg

Editor **Sally Harding**
Designer **Heather Johns**
Knitting Pattern Checker **Marilyn Wilson**
Knitting Charts and Diagrams **Dennis Wilson**
Photographer **Trevor Leighton**
Models **Jane Crossley, Dawn French and Sharon Henry**
Stylist **Susie Slack**
Hair **Keith Harris**
Make-up **Charlie Duffy**
Photographer's Assistant **Adrian Sanders**

First published by Century in 1990.
This paperback edition published in 1991
by Century, an imprint of
Random Century Group Limited,
Random Century House,
20 Vauxhall Bridge Road,
London SW1V 2SA

Random Century Australia Pty Ltd,
20 Alfred Street, Milsons Point,
Sydney 2061, Australia

Random Century (NZ) Ltd,
18 Poland Road, Glenfield,
Auckland 10, New Zealand

Random Century South Africa Pty Ltd,
PO Box 337, Bergvlei, 2012 South Africa

A catalogue record for this book is
available from the British Library

ISBN 0 7126 5097 0

Phototypeset by SX Composing Ltd, Rayleigh, Essex
Printed and bound in Singapore

CONTENTS

INTRODUCTION

Aren't knitwear books dreadful?!

If anyone had asked me a year ago whether I would like to be involved with a book about knitting patterns, I would have laughed so long and hard that something tragic would have taken place in my underpants.

This year, three important things have happened:
First, I tried to buy a sweater only to discover that the biggest size available in the styles I liked would only have fitted a beanshoot with anorexia. Secondly, I met Sylvie Soudan. Thirdly, I became a virgin at long last, but that is personal and nothing to do with this book.

Unlike most knitwear designers who appear to have done their apprenticeships with only chilly stick insects in mind, Sylvie appreciates the desire many women have to wear knitwear that is loose and comfortable. For the 'ampler', more gorgeous woman, she is a godsend. A lot of big girls who venture out to purchase knitwear very soon give up in despair, and spend the money on big cream cakes and boxes of Kleenex to sob into. Now, I'm not averse to the odd presentation box of cream cakes myself but I'd kill to have the opportunity to eat them while I'm snuggled up in my fab new woolly. As for pregnant women – they're gasping for help – they don't want *drugs*, they want knits that *fit*.

Well, here it is, a first. A book of big, beautiful knitwear for big, beautiful women. We decided not to use professional models in the book (although it has to be said that my likeness to Jerry Hall is uncanny in these pages) and so the other two girls are Sharon Henry, my sister-in-law, and Jane Crossley, Sylvie's friend. I thought it would be a good idea to show how these knits look on ordinary women with no modelling experience. Since this book, needless to say, we have all been signed up to strut the classiest catwalks of the fashion world. (To check them for sturdiness and safety, admittedly, but it's a start . . .)

There are designs for everyone in this book. Even thinner women can look good in these knits, bless them.

I hope you enjoy the book and I hope you enjoy the sweaters more. Stay warm!

DAWN FRENCH
August 1989

SUMMER COTTONS

Here are four cotton designs to wake up your wardrobe. Knitted in Rowan Yarn's lovely _Handknit DK_, these bold creations in crisp navy and white will always look stunning wherever the sun is.

SHELLS

ROWAN HANDKNIT DK COTTON

SIZE
One size only (see page 118 for choosing size)
Finished measurement around bust 170cm (68")
See diagram for finished measurements of back, front and sleeves. To lengthen or shorten back and front, or sleeves see page 118.

MATERIALS
Rowan *Handknit DK Cotton*
17 x 50g (1¾oz) balls in Ecru (shade no. 251) A
5 x 50g (1¾oz) balls in Navy (shade no. 277) B
One pair each 3¼mm (US size 3) and 4mm (US size 6) needles *or size to obtain correct tension (gauge)*

TENSION (GAUGE)
20 sts and 28 rows to 10cm (4") over st st on 4mm (US size 6) needles
Check your tension (gauge) before beginning.

NOTES
Do not strand yarns across back of work, but use a separate ball of yarn for each isolated area of colour, twisting yarns at back when changing colours to avoid holes.
Read charts from right to left for RS (knit) rows and from left to right for WS (purl) rows.

BACK
Using smaller needles and yarn A, cast on 170 sts.
Beg K2, P2 twisted rib as foll:
1st rib row (RS) K2 tbl, *P2, K2 tbl, rep from * to end.
2nd rib row P2, *K2 tbl, P2, rep from * to end.
Rep last 2 rows, until ribbing measures 5cm (2") from beg, ending with a RS row.
Change to larger needles and P one row.
Beg with first chart row (K row), work in st st foll chart for back (see *Notes* above) until 72nd chart row has been completed, so ending with a WS row.
Shape Raglans
Cont to foll chart for colour patt throughout, cast (bind) off 5 sts at beg of next 2 rows. 160 sts.
Dec one st at each end of next and every foll alt row 26 times in all. 108 sts.
Dec one st at each end of every row 17 times, so ending with a WS row. 74 sts.
Shape Neck
Beg neck shaping for back neck on next row as foll:

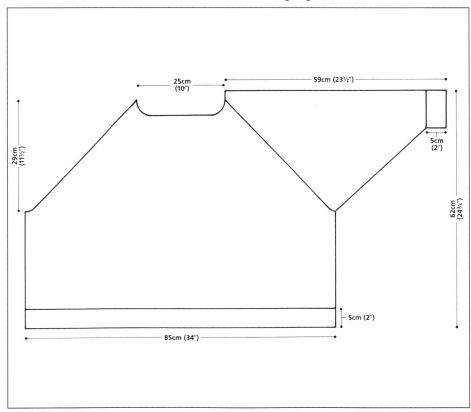

25cm (10")   59cm (23½")   5cm (2")   29cm (11½")   62cm (24¾")   5cm (2")   85cm (34")

Inspired by a holiday in France, this sweater is knitted in double knit cotton with deep raglan sleeves, finished with a blanket stitch detail.

'Simple shape and a bold design. A firm favourite!'

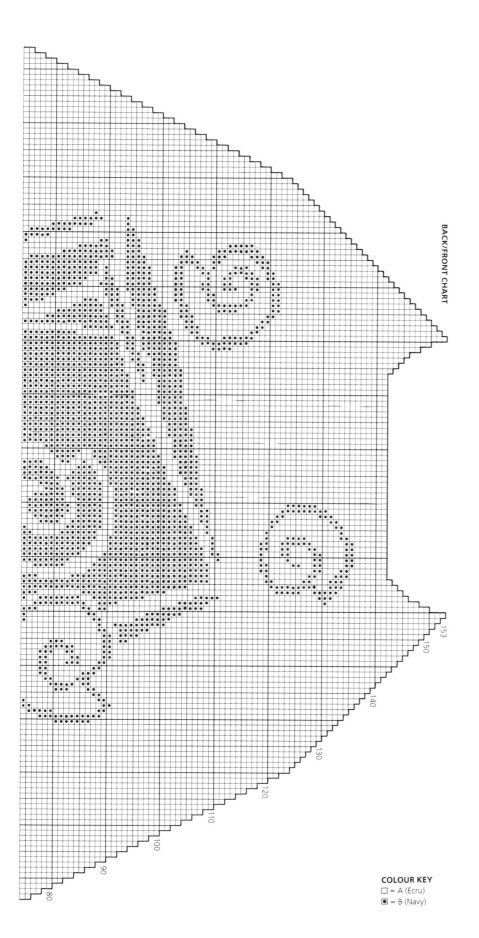

BACK/FRONT CHART

COLOUR KEY
□ = A (Ecru)
▣ = B (Navy)

Next row (RS) Sl 1-K1-psso, K16, turn leaving rem sts on a spare needle.

Working on first side of neck only, **dec one st at each end of next 4 rows.

Dec one st at armhole edge only on next row. Then cont raglan shaping by dec one st at armhole edge on every row *and at the same time* dec one st at neck edge on next row and foll alt row. 3 sts. Dec one st at armhole edge on next 2 rows.

Fasten off rem st.**

Return to rem sts and with RS facing, slip centre 38 sts onto a st holder, rejoin yarn to rem sts and K to last 2 sts, K2tog.

Rep from ** to ** of first side of neck.

FRONT

Work as for Back.

SLEEVES

Using smaller needles and yarn A, cast on 50 sts.

Work 5cm (2") in twisted rib patt as for Back, ending with a 2nd row.

Change to larger needles and beg with a K row, work 2 rows in st st.

Cont in st st, inc one st at each end of next and every foll alt row 9 times in all. 68 sts.

Then beg with 20th chart row, work in st st foll sleeve chart *and at the same time* cont shaping Sleeve by inc one st at each end of every alt row until there are 116 sts.

Cont to foll chart for colour patt throughout, work 3 rows without shaping, so ending with WS row.

Shape Raglans

Cast (bind) off 5 sts at beg of next 2 rows. 106 sts.

Dec one st at each end of next and every foll alt row 30 times in all. 46 sts.

Dec one st at each end of every row 19 times.

Cast (bind) off rem 8 sts.

Make 2nd Sleeve in same way.

SLEEVE CHART

COLOUR KEY
☐ = A (Ecru)
▣ = B (Navy)

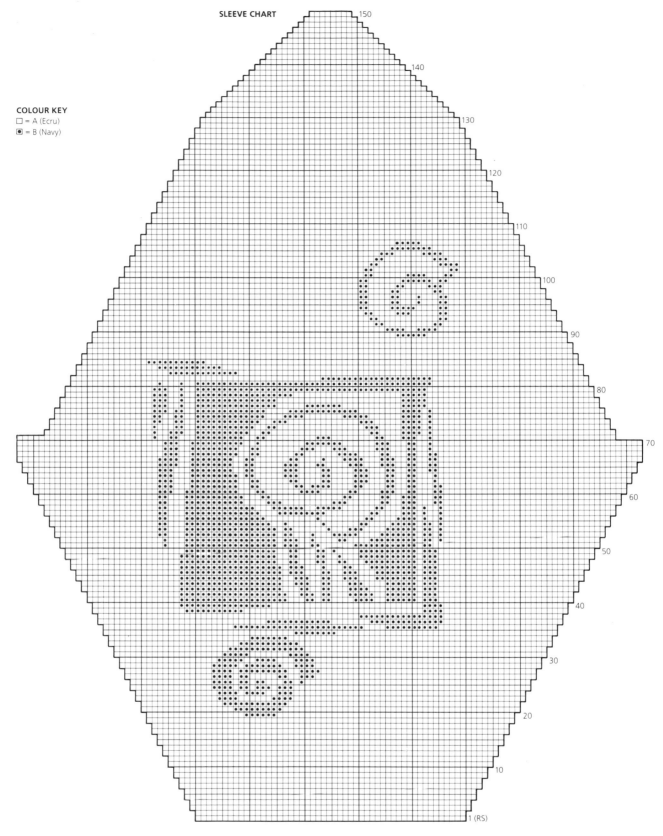

COLLAR

Press pieces lightly on WS with a warm iron over a damp cloth, omitting ribbing.

Join Sleeves to Back and Front at raglan edges, leaving left back seam open.

Then after 3 raglan seams have been joined, work Collar as foll:
Using smaller needles and yarn A and with RS facing, pick up and K8 sts across left sleeve top, 8 sts down left front neck, K38 sts from st holder, pick up and K8 sts up right front neck, 8 sts across right sleeve top, 8 sts down right back neck, K38 sts from st holder and pick up and K8 sts up left back neck. 124 sts.

Work 5cm (2") in K2, P2 twisted rib.

Cast (bind) off in rib.

FINISHING

Join left back raglan seam and collar. Join side and sleeve seams.

Blanket Stitch Edging

Using yarn B double, work blanket stitch (see page 121) around lower rib, cuffs and collar the depth of the rib, i.e. 5cm (2"). Press seams lightly on WS with a warm iron over a damp cloth, omitting ribbing.

GONE FISHING

ROWAN HANDKNIT DK COTTON

SIZE

One size only (see page 118 for choosing size)
Finished measurement around bust 170cm (68")
See diagram for finished measurements of back, front and sleeves. To lengthen or shorten back and front, or sleeves see page 118.

MATERIALS

Rowan *Handknit DK Cotton*
17 x 50g (1¾oz) balls in Ecru (shade no. 251) A
5 x 50g (1¾oz) balls in Navy (shade no. 277) B
One pair each 3¼mm (US size 3) and 4mm (US size 6) needles *or size to obtain correct tension (gauge)*

TENSION (GAUGE)

20 sts and 28 rows to 10cm (4") over st st on 4mm (US size 6) needles
Check your tension (gauge) before beginning.

NOTES

When working S-motif colourwork band with yarns A and B, carry colour not in use across back of work weaving it around working yarn. When working fish motifs, carry yarn A across entire row weaving it around yarn B at back when not in use, but use a separate ball of yarn B for each isolated area of colour, twisting yarns at back when changing colours to avoid holes.
Read charts from right to left for RS (knit) rows and from left to right for WS (purl) rows.
All ribbing is worked in ordinary K2, P2 rib; if a firmer ribbing is desired, use twisted K2, P2 rib as
for Shells *sweater on page 10.*

BACK

Using smaller needles and yarn B, cast on 170 sts.
K one row (RS).
Change to yarn A and beg K2, P2 rib (see *Notes* above) as foll:
1st rib row (WS) K2, *P2, K2, rep from * to end.
2nd rib row P2, *K2, P2, rep from * to end.
Rep last 2 rows, until ribbing measures 5cm (2") from beg, ending with a WS row.
Change to larger needles and beg with first chart row (K row), work in st st foll chart for back (see *Notes* above) until 74th chart row has been completed, so ending with a WS row.

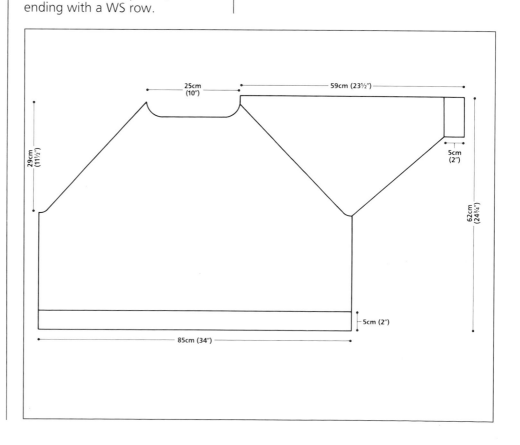

Shape Raglans

Cont to foll chart for colour patt throughout, cast (bind) off 5 sts at beg of next 2 rows. 160 sts.
Dec one st at each end of next and every foll alt row 26 times in all. 108 sts.
Dec one st at each end of every row 17 times, so with a WS row. 74 sts.

Shape Neck

Beg neck shaping on next row as foll:

Next row (RS) Sl 1-K1-psso, K16, turn leaving rem sts on a spare needle.
Working on first side of neck only, **dec one st at each end of next 4 rows.
Dec one st at armhole edge only on next row. Then cont raglan shaping by dec one st at armhole edge on every row *and at the same time* dec one st at neck edge on next row and foll alt row. 3 sts. Dec one st at armhole edge on next 2 rows.
Fasten off rem st.**
Return to rem sts and with RS facing, slip centre 38 sts onto a st holder, rejoin yarn to rem sts and K to last 2 sts, K2tog.
Rep from ** to ** of first side of

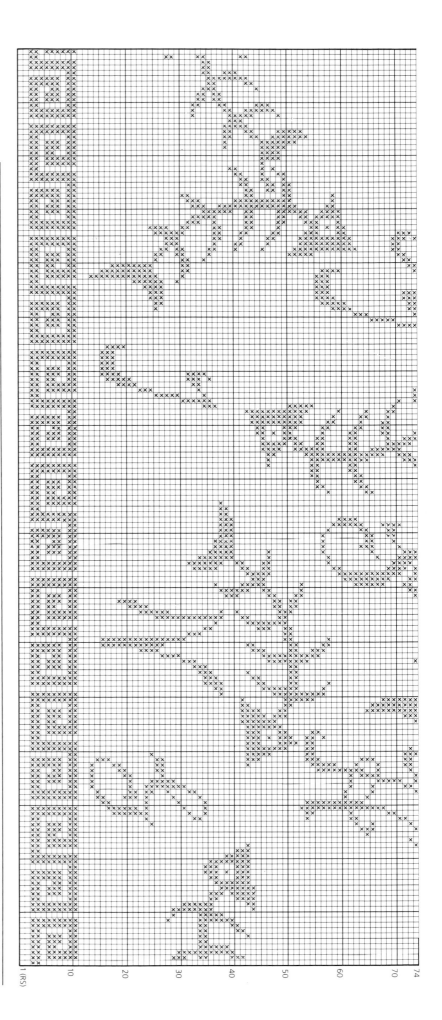

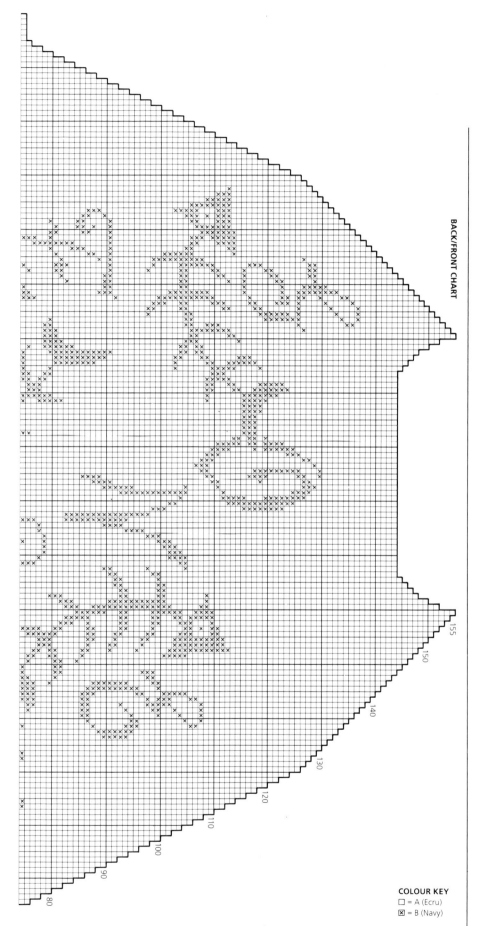

BACK/FRONT CHART

155
150
140
130
120
110
100
90
80

COLOUR KEY
□ = A (Ecru)
☒ = B (Navy)

neck to complete 2nd side.

FRONT
Work as for Back.

SLEEVES
Using smaller needles and yarn B, cast on 50 sts.
K one row (RS).
Change to yarn A and work K2, P2 rib as for Back until ribbing measures 5cm (2") from beg, ending with a WS row.
Change to larger needles and beg with a K row, work 2 rows in st st.
Beg with 3rd chart row, work in st st foll sleeve chart *and at the same time* shape Sleeve by inc one st at each end of next and every foll alt row until there are 116 sts.
Cont to foll chart for colour patt throughout, work 3 rows without shaping, so ending with a WS row.
Shape Raglans
Cast (bind) off 5 sts at beg of next 2 rows. 106 sts.
Dec one st at each end of next and every foll alt row 30 times in all. 46 sts.
Dec one st at each end of every

A variation on a water theme, this garment is illustrated with fishbones and lettering to create a stylish sweater with an intriguing design.

'A cotton knit with a puzzle to solve to boot! It will keep the bus queue amused for hours.'

SLEEVE CHART

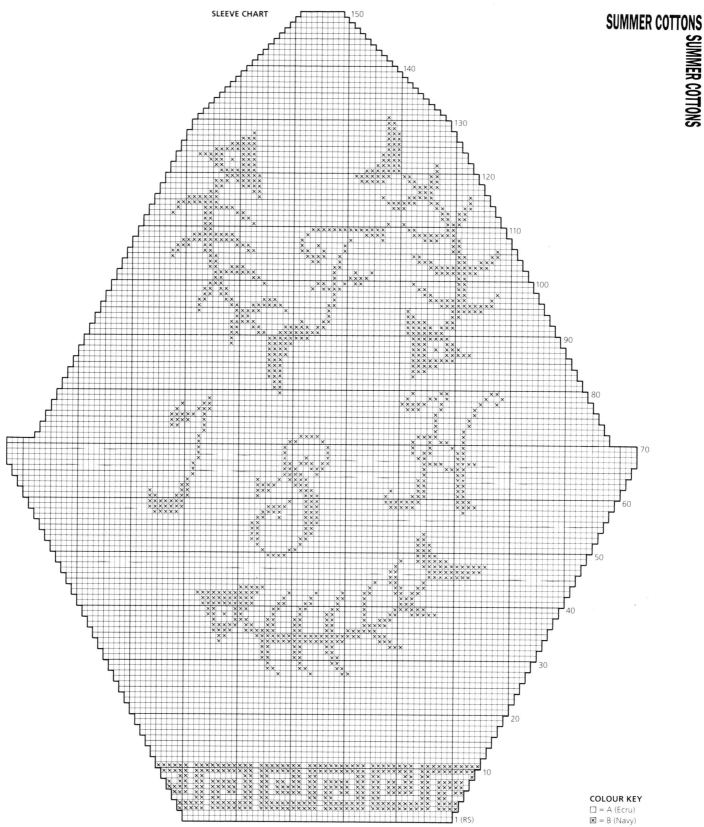

150
140
130
120
110
100
90
80
70
60
50
40
30
20
10
1 (RS)

COLOUR KEY
□ = A (Ecru)
☒ = B (Navy)

foll row 19 times to complete. Cast (bind) off rem 8 sts. Make 2nd Sleeve in the same way.

COLLAR
Press pieces lightly on WS with a warm iron over a damp cloth, omitting ribbing.
Join the Sleeves to Back and Front at the raglan edges, leaving the left back seam open.
Using smaller needles and yarn A and with RS facing, pick up and K8 sts across left sleeve top, 8 sts down left front neck, K38 sts from st holder, pick up and K8 sts up right front neck, 8 sts across right sleeve top, 8 sts down right back neck, K38 sts from st holder and pick up and K8 sts up left back neck. 124 sts.

Work 5cm (2") in K2, P2 rib, working last 2 rows in yarn B. Using yarn B, cast (bind) off in rib.

FINISHING
Join left back raglan seam and collar. Join side and sleeve seams. Press lightly on WS with a warm iron over a damp cloth, omitting ribbing.

JAPANESE FISH

ROWAN HANDKNIT DK COTTON

SIZE
One size only (see page 118 for choosing size)
Finished measurement around bust 170cm (68")
See diagram for finished measurements of back, front and sleeves. To lengthen or shorten back and front, or sleeves see page 118.

MATERIALS
Rowan *Handknit DK Cotton*
19 x 50g (1¾oz) balls Ecru (shade no. 251) A
4 x 50g (1¾oz) balls of Navy (shade no. 277) B
One pair each 3¼mm (US size 3) and 4mm (US size 6) needles *or size to obtain correct tension (gauge)*

TENSION (GAUGE)
20 sts and 28 rows to 10cm (4") over st st on 4mm (US size 6) needles
Check your tension (gauge) before beginning.

NOTES
When using 2 colours in a row, carry yarn A across entire row weaving it around yarn B when not in use, but use a separate ball of yarn B for each isolated area of colour, twisting yarns at back when changing colours to avoid holes.
Read charts from right to left for RS (knit) rows and from left to right for WS (purl) rows.

BACK
Using smaller needles and yarn B, cast on 170 sts.
K one row (RS).
Change to yarn A and beg K2, P2 twisted rib as foll:
1st rib row (WS) K2 tbl, *P2, K2

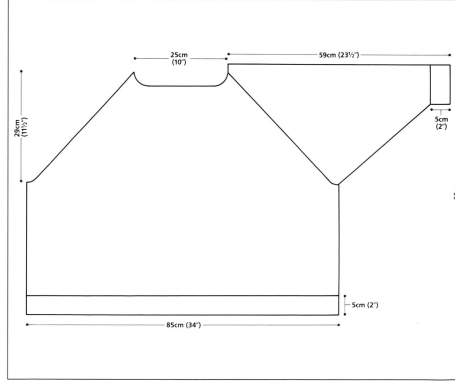

25cm (10") 59cm (23½") 29cm (11½") 5cm (2") 66cm 5cm (2") 85cm (34")

This lovely fish was in-
spired by a Japanese sten-
cil dating from 1880. A
sophisticated cotton
sweater with deep raglans
for style and ease of move-
ment.

*'An Oriental idea. (Sylvie's
obviously been having some
expensive holidays for this
sort of inspiration.)'*

tbl, rep from * to end.

2nd rib row P2, *K2 tbl, P2, rep from * to end.

Rep last 2 rows, until ribbing measures 5cm (2") from beg, ending with a WS row.

Change to larger needles and beg with first chart row (K row), work in st st foll chart for back (see *Notes* above) until 84th chart row has been completed, so ending with a WS row.

Shape Raglans

Cont to foll chart for colour patt throughout, cast (bind) off 5 sts at beg of next 2 rows. 160 sts.

Dec one st at each end of next and every foll alt row 26 times in all. 108 sts.

Dec one st at each end of every row 17 times, so ending with a WS row. 74 sts.

Shape Neck

Beg neck shaping on next row as foll:

Next row (RS) Sl 1-K1-psso, K16, turn leaving rem sts on a spare needle.

Working on first side of neck only, **dec one st at each end of next 4 rows.

Dec one st at armhole edge only on next row. Then cont raglan shaping by dec one st at armhole edge on every row *and at the same time* dec one st at neck edge on next row and foll alt row. 3 sts. Dec one st at armhole edge on next 2 rows.

Fasten off rem st.**

Return to rem sts and with RS

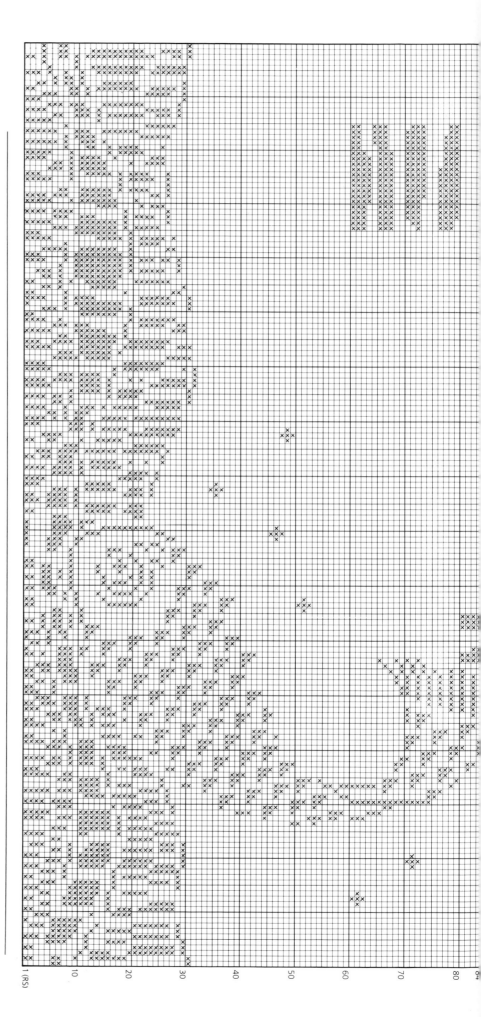

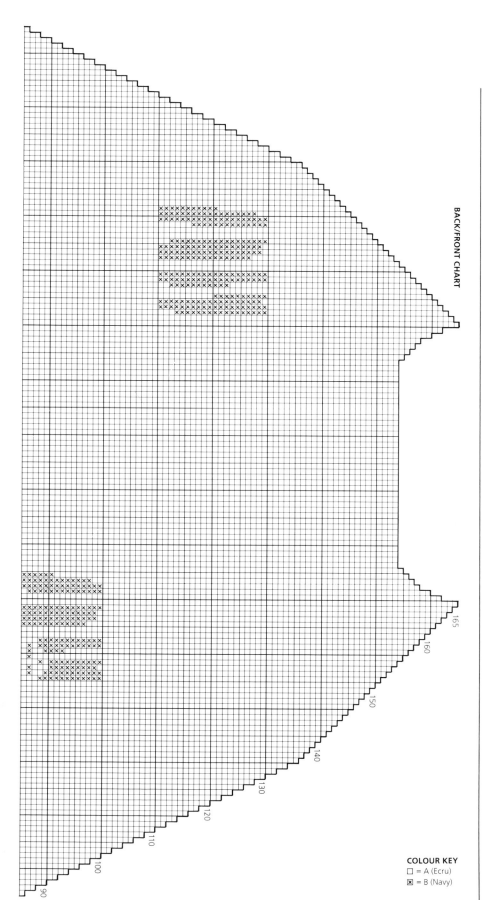

BACK/FRONT CHART

COLOUR KEY
□ = A (Ecru)
☒ = B (Navy)

facing, slip centre 38 sts onto a st holder, rejoin yarn to rem sts and K to last 2 sts, K2tog.
Rep from ** to ** of first side of neck to complete 2nd side.

FRONT
Work as for Back.

SLEEVES
Using smaller needles and yarn B, cast on 50 sts.
K one row (RS).
Change to yarn A and then work in the twisted rib patt as for the Back until the ribbing measures 5cm (2") from the beg, ending with a WS row.
Change to larger needles and beg with a K row, work 2 rows in st st.
Cont in st st, inc one st at each end of next and every foll alt row 12 times in all. 74 sts.
Then beg with 26th chart row, work in st st foll sleeve chart *and at the same time* cont shaping Sleeve by inc one st at each end of every alt row until there are 116 sts.
Cont to foll chart for colour patt throughout, work 3 rows without shaping, so ending with a WS row.
Shape Raglans
Cast (bind) off 5 sts at beg of next 2 rows. 106 sts.
Dec one st at each end of next and every foll alt row 30 times in all. 46 sts.
Dec one st at each end of every

SLEEVE CHART

COLOUR KEY
☐ = A (Ecru)
☒ = B (Navy)

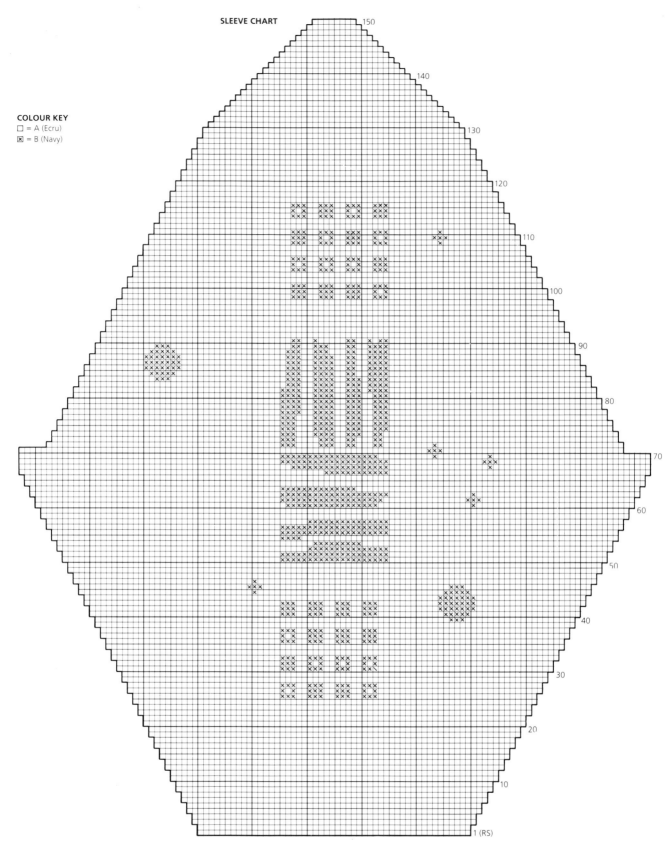

foll row 19 times to complete.
Cast (bind) off rem 8 sts.
Make 2nd Sleeve in the same
way.

COLLAR
Press pieces lightly on WS with a
warm iron over a damp cloth,
omitting ribbing.
Join the Sleeves to the Back and
Front at the raglan edges, leaving

the left back seam open.
Using smaller needles and yarn A
and with RS facing, pick up and
K8 sts across left sleeve top, 8 sts
down left front neck, K38 sts
from st holder, pick up and K8
sts up right front neck, 8 sts
across right sleeve top, 8 sts
down right back neck, K38 sts
from st holder and pick up and
K8 sts up left back neck. 124 sts.

Work 5cm (2") in K2, P2 twisted
rib, working last row in yarn B.
Using yarn B, cast (bind) off
in rib.

FINISHING
Join left back raglan seam and
collar. Join side and sleeve seams.
Press seams lightly on WS with a
warm iron over a damp cloth,
omitting ribbing.

NAUTICAL

R O W A N   H A N D K N I T   D K   C O T T O N

SIZE

One size only (see page 118 for choosing size)
Finished measurement around bust 158cm (63")
See diagram for finished measurements of back, front and sleeves. To lengthen or shorten back and front, or sleeves see page 118.

MATERIALS

Rowan *Handknit DK Cotton*
9 x 50g (1¾oz) balls in Ecru (shade no. 251) A
9 x 50g (1¾oz) balls in Navy (shade no. 277) B
3 x 50g (1¾oz) balls in Cherry (shade no. 298) C
One pair each 3¼mm (US size 3) and 4mm (US size 6) needles *or size to obtain correct tension (gauge)*

TENSION (GAUGE)

20 sts and 28 rows to 10cm (4") over st st on 4mm (US size 6) needles
Check your tension (gauge) before beginning.

NOTES

When working stripes, do not break off yarn after each stripe (unless stated otherwise), but drop yarn at side of work ready to be used again, so that yarn is carried loosely up side of work as colours are alternated.
When working motif, do not strand yarn C across back of work, but use a separate length of yarn for each isolated area of colour, twisting yarns at back when changing colours to avoid holes.
Read chart from right to left for RS (knit) rows and from left to right for WS (purl) rows.

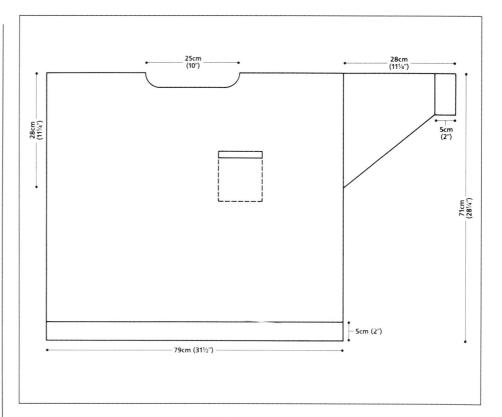

BACK

Using smaller needles and yarn A, cast on 158 sts.
Knit one row (RS).
Change to yarn B and beg K1, P1 twisted rib as foll:
1st rib row (WS) *K1 tbl, P1, rep from * to end.
Rep last row 10 times more.
Change to larger needles and using yarn A and beg with a K row, work 6 rows in st st.
Cont in st st throughout, work 6 rows in yarn B.
Work 12 rows in yarn C. Break off C.
Work 6 rows in yarn A, then work 6 rows in yarn B.**
Rep last 12 rows 11 times more, so ending with 6 rows in yarn B.
Work 4 rows in yarn A, so ending with a WS row.

Shape Neck

Keeping to stripe patt of 6 rows A and 6 rows B throughout, beg the neck shaping on the next row as foll:
Next row (RS) K60, turn leaving rem sts on a spare needle.
Working on first side of neck only, dec one st at neck edge on every row 4 times, then dec one st at neck edge on 2 foll alt rows. 54 sts.
Work 3 rows in stripe patt without shaping.
Cast (bind) off.
Return to rem sts and with RS facing, slip centre 38 sts onto a st holder, rejoin yarn to rem sts and K to end.
Complete 2nd side of neck to match first side, reversing all of the shaping.

FRONT
Before beg Front, make pocket lining.
Pocket Lining
Using larger needles and A, cast on 22 sts.
Work in st st until lining measures 10cm (4") from beg.
Break off yarn and slip sts onto a st holder to be used later.
Work Front as for Back to **.
Rep last 12 rows 7 times more, so ending with 6 rows in yarn B.
Work 6 rows in yarn A, then 2 rows in yarn B, so ending with a WS row.
Place Pocket
Keeping to stripe of 6 rows A and 6 rows B, place pocket on next row as foll:
Next row (RS) K45, slip next 22 sts onto a st holder, K the 22 sts of pocket lining from the st holder, K to end.
Complete as for Back.

SLEEVES
Using smaller needles and yarn A, cast on 52 sts.
Knit one row (RS).
Change to yarn B and work 11 rows in K1, P1 twisted rib as for Back.
Change to larger needles and using yarn B and beg with a K row, work 2 rows in st st.
Knit one row in yarn A, inc one st at each end of row.
Purl one row in yarn A.
Knit one row in yarn B, inc one st at each end of row.
Purl one row in yarn B.
Rep last 4 rows 6 times more, so ending with 2 rows in yarn B. 80 sts.
Cont in st st throughout and cont to inc one st at each end of next and every foll alt row, work 3 rows in A, so ending with a RS row. 84 sts.
Place position of motif (see *Notes* above) on next row as foll:
Next row (WS) P39 in yarn A, P6 in yarn C, P39 in yarn A.
The position of the motif is now set.
Cont inc one st at each end of next and every foll alt row *and at the same time* beg with 3rd chart row (K row), cont in st st foll the motif chart and working the background in yarn A until 16th chart row has been completed, so ending with a WS row. 98 sts.
Cont inc one st at each end of next and every foll alt row *and at the same time* work the last 4 rows of the motif, but working in yarn C on both sides of the chart, so that the 4 rows of C form a stripe around the Sleeve, so ending with a WS row. 102 sts.
Cont inc one st at each end of next and every foll alt row, (work 2 rows in yarn A, 2 rows in yarn B) twice, then work 2 rows in yarn C. 112 sts.
Work 2 rows in yarn C without shaping.
Cast (bind) off all sts.
Make the 2nd Sleeve in the same way as the first.

NECKBAND
Press pieces lightly on WS with a warm iron over a damp cloth, omitting ribbing.
Join right shoulder seam.
Using smaller needles and yarn C and with RS facing, pick up and K11 sts down left front neck, K38 sts from st holder, pick up and K11 sts up right front neck, 11 sts down right back neck, K38 sts from back neck st holder and pick up and K11 sts up left back neck. 120 sts.
Work 10 rows in rib as for Back.
Change to yarn A and rib one row.
Using yarn A, cast (bind) off in rib.

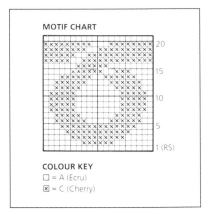

MOTIF CHART

20

15

10

5

1 (RS)

COLOUR KEY
☐ = A (Ecru)
☒ = C (Cherry)

FINISHING
Join left shoulder seam and neckband.
Pocket Top
Using smaller needles and yarn C and with RS facing, K22 sts across pocket top from st holder.
Work 5 rows in K1, P1 twisted rib as for Back. Change to yarn A and rib one row. Using yarn A, cast (bind) off.
Sew pocket top to RS and sew pocket lining to WS.
Place markers on Back and Front 28cm (11¼") from shoulder seam.
Sew Sleeves to Back and Front between markers.
Join side and sleeve seams.
Press seams lightly on WS with a warm iron over a damp cloth, omitting ribbing.

Every wardrobe should have a simple navy and white striped sweater; it never dates and always looks fresh and classic. This design includes a touch of red, French style.

'Who says big girls can't wear horizontal stripes? Ha! Ha!'

SOPHISTICATED CLASSICS

Build up your wardrobe with these essential classics. Dress them up or wear them plain, they will fit in equally well at the office or out on the town. Knit one and you'll want to team it up with another.

CHILLI CARDIGAN

ROWAN SILKSTONES

SIZE
One size only (see page 118 for choosing size)
Finished measurement around bust 131cm (52½")
See diagram for finished measurements of back, fronts and sleeves. To lengthen or shorten back and fronts, or sleeves see page 118.

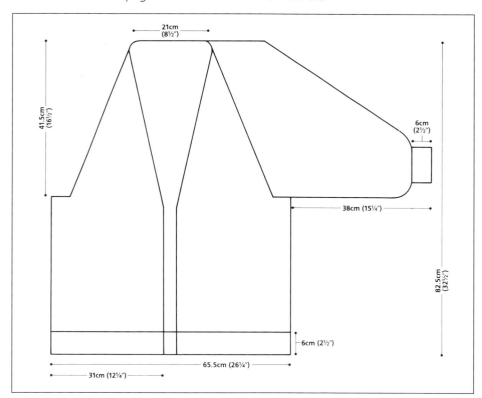

21cm (8½")
41.5cm (16½")
6cm (2½")
38cm (15¼")
82.5cm (32½")
6cm (2½")
65.5cm (26¼")
31cm (12¼")

MATERIALS
10 x 50g (1¾oz) balls of Rowan *Silkstones* in Chilli (shade no. 826)
One pair each 3¼mm (US size 3) and 4mm (US size 6) needles *or size to obtain correct tension (gauge)*
Five 2cm (¾") buttons
One stitch marker

TENSION (GAUGE)
24 sts and 28 rows to 10cm (4") over st st on 4mm (US size 6) needles
Check your tension (gauge) before beginning.

BACK
Using smaller needles, cast on 157 sts.
1st rib row (RS) K1, *P1, K1, rep from * to end.
2nd rib row P1, *K1, P1, rep from * to end.
Cont to rep first and 2nd rib rows until ribbing measures 6cm (2½") from beg, ending with a WS row.
Change to larger needles and beg with a K row, work in st st until Back measures 41cm (16")

from beg, ending with a WS row.
Shape Raglans
Cont in st st, cast (bind) off 15 sts at beg of next 2 rows. 127 sts.
Beg the raglan shaping on the next row as foll:
**1st row (RS) P2, (K1 tbl, P1) twice, sl 1-K1-psso, K to last 8 sts, K2 tog, (P1, K1 tbl) twice, P2.
2nd row K2, (P1, K1) twice, P to last 6 sts, (K1, P1) twice, K2.
3rd row P2, (K1 tbl, P1) twice, K1 tbl, K to last 7 sts, K1 tbl, (P1, K1 tbl) twice, P2.
4th row K2, (P1, K1) twice, P2 tog, P to last 8 sts, P2 tog tbl, (K1, P1) twice, K2.
5th row As 3rd row.
6th row As 2nd row.**
Rep first-6th rows just worked (from ** to **) until 51 sts rem and ending with a 6th row (WS).
Cast (bind) off all sts in patt.

LEFT FRONT
Using smaller needles, cast on 74 sts.
Work 6cm (2½") in K1, P1 rib, ending with a WS row.
Change to larger needles and beg with a K row, work in st st until there are 10 rows less than Back to armhole shaping and Back measures approx 37.5cm (14½") from beg, so ending with a WS row.***
Shape V-neck
Cont in st st, beg neck shaping as foll:
Next row (RS) K to last 3 sts, K2 tog, K1.
Work 5 rows in st st without shaping, so ending with a WS row.
Next row (RS) K to last 3 sts, K2 tog, K1. 72 sts.
Begin with a P row, work 3 rows in st st without shaping, so ending with a WS row.

This wool and silk cardi-
gan, sweater and skirt with
their fine light texture can
be worn all year round. Very
flattering shapes whatever
your size.

*'Not the kind of cardi your
mum made, this one is part
silk. Eat your heart out.
They look tasty and
they're hot to handle!'*

Shape Raglan
Next row (RS) Cast (bind) off 15 sts, K to end. 57 sts.
Purl one row.
Beg raglan shaping as foll:
1st row (RS) P2, (K1 tbl, P1) twice, sl 1-K1-psso, K to last 3 sts, K2 tog, K1.
2nd row P to last 6 sts, (K1, P1) twice, K2.
3rd row P2, (K1 tbl, P1) twice, K1 tbl, K to end.
4th row P to last 8 sts, P2 tog tbl, (K1, P1) twice, K2.
5th row As 3rd row.
6th row As 2nd row.
Rep first-6th rows just worked until 9 sts rem, so ending with a 4th row (WS).
Next row (RS) P2, (K1 tbl, P1) twice, K1 tbl, K2 tog.

Next row P2, (K1, P1) twice, K2.
Next row P2, (K1 tbl, P1) twice, sl 1-K1-psso.
Next row K2 tog, P1, K1, P1, K2.
Next row P2, K1 tbl, P3 tog. 4 sts.
Cast (bind) off in patt.

RIGHT FRONT
Work as for Left Front to ***.
Shape V-neck
Cont in st st, beg neck shaping as foll:
Next row (RS) K1, sl 1-K1-psso, K to end.
Work 5 rows in st st without shaping, so ending with a WS row.
Next row (RS) K1, sl 1-K1-psso, K to end. 72 sts.
Work 4 rows in st st without

shaping, so ending with a RS row.
Shape Raglan
Next row (WS) Cast (bind) off 15 sts, P to end. 57 sts.
Beg raglan shaping as foll:
1st row (RS) K1, sl 1-K1-psso, K to last 8 sts, K2 tog, (P1, K1 tbl) twice, P2.
2nd row K2, (P1, K1) twice, P to end.
3rd row K to last 7 sts, K1 tbl, (P1, K1 tbl) twice, P2.
4th row K2, (P1, K1) twice, P2 tog, P to end.
5th row As 3rd row.
6th row As 2nd row.
Rep first-6th rows just worked until 9 sts rem, so ending with a 4th row (WS).
Next row (RS) K2 tog, K1 tbl, (P1, K1 tbl) twice, P2.
Next row K2, (P1, K1) twice, P2.
Next row K2 tog, (P1, K1 tbl) twice, P2.
Next row K2, P1, K1, P1, K2 tog.
Next row K2 tog, P1, K1 tbl, P2.
Next row K2, P1, K2 tog. 4 sts.
Cast (bind) off in patt.

RIGHT SLEEVE
Using smaller needles, cast on 55 sts.
Work 6cm (2½") in K1, P1 rib as for Back, ending with a WS row and inc in each st across last row. 110 sts.
Change to larger needles and beg with a K row, work in st st inc one st at each end of 3rd and every foll 3rd row until there are 168 sts, so ending with a RS row.
Work 3 rows in st st without shaping, so ending with a WS row.
Shape Raglans
Cont in st st, cast (bind) off 15 sts at beg of next 2 rows. 138 sts.
Work as for Back from ** to **.
Rep first-6th rows just worked until 90 sts rem and ending with a 6th row (WS). Place st marker between 45th and 46th st.
Shape Shoulder
Beg shaping shoulder at centre of Sleeve on next row as foll:

1st row (RS) P2, (K1 tbl, P1) twice, sl 1-K1-psso, K to within 2 sts of centre marker, sl 1-K1-psso, slip marker onto right-hand needle, K2 tog, K to last 8 sts, K2 tog, (P1, K1 tbl) twice, P2. (4 sts decreased.)
2nd row K2, (P1, K1) twice, P to last 6 sts (always slipping marker when it is reached on each row), (K1, P1) twice, K2.
3rd row P2, (K1 tbl, P1) twice, K1 tbl, K to last 7 sts, K1 tbl, (P1, K1 tbl) twice, P2.
4th row (WS) K2, (P1, K1) twice, P2 tog, P to within 2 sts of centre marker, P2 tog, P2 tog tbl, P to last 8 sts, P2 tog tbl, (K1, P1) twice, K2. (4 sts decreased.)
5th row As 3rd row.
6th row As 2nd row.
Rep first-6th rows just worked until 50 sts rem and ending with a 5th row (RS).
Neck Shaping
Beg neck shaping on next row as foll:****
Next row (WS) K2, (P1, K1) twice, P to last 6 sts, (K1, P1) twice, K2 tog.
Mark end of last row with a coloured thread to indicate beg of neck shaping.
Next row K2 tog, P1, K1 tbl, P1, sl 1-K1-psso, K to within 2 sts of centre marker, sl 1-K1-psso, K2 tog, K to last 8 sts, K2 tog, (P1, K1 tbl) twice, P2.
Next row K2, (P1, K1) twice, P to last 4 sts, K1, P1, K2 tog.
Next row K2 tog, P1, K1 tbl, K to last 7 sts, K1 tbl, (P1, K1 tbl) twice, P2.
Next row K2, (P1, K1) twice, P2 tog, P to within 2 sts of centre marker, P2 tog, P2 tog tbl, P to last 4 sts, P2 tog tbl, K2 tog.
Next row K2 tog, K to last 7 sts, K1 tbl, (P1, K1 tbl) twice, P2.
Next row K2, (P1, K1) twice, P to last 2 sts, P2 tog.
Next row Cast (bind) off 5 sts, K to within 2 sts of centre marker, sl 1-K1-psso, K2 tog, K to last 8 sts, K2 tog, (P1, K1 tbl) twice, P2.
Next row K2, (P1, K1) twice,

P to the end of the row.
Next row Cast (bind) off 5 sts, K to last 7 sts, K1 tbl, (P1, K1 tbl) twice, P2.
Next row K2, (P1, K1) twice, P2 tog, P to within 2 sts of centre marker, P2 tog, P2 tog tbl, P1.
Next row Cast (bind) off 5 sts, K to last 7 sts, K1 tbl, (P1, K1 tbl) twice, P2. 14 sts.
Next row K2, (P1, K1) twice, P to end.
Cast (bind) off in patt.

LEFT SLEEVE
Work as for Right Sleeve to ****.
Next row (WS) K2 tog, (P1, K1) twice, P to last 6 sts, (K1, P1) twice, K2.
Mark beg of last row with a coloured thread to indicate beg of neck shaping.
Next row P2, (K1 tbl, P1) twice, sl 1-K1-psso, K to within 2 sts of centre marker, sl 1-K1-psso, K2 tog, K to last 7 sts, K2 tog, P1, K1 tbl, P1, K2 tog.
Next row K2 tog, P1, K1, P to last 6 sts, (K1, P1) twice, K2.
Next row P2, (K1 tbl, P1) twice, K1 tbl, K to last 4 sts, K1 tbl, P1, K2 tog.
Next row K2 tog, P2 tog, P to within 2 sts of centre marker, P2 tog, P2 tog tbl, P to last 8 sts, P2 tog tbl, (K1, P1) twice, K2.
Next row P2, (K1 tbl, P1) twice, K1 tbl, K to last 2 sts, K2 tog.
Next row P2 tog, P to last 6 sts, (K1, P1) twice, K2.
Next row P2, (K1 tbl, P1) twice, sl 1-K1-psso, K to within 2 sts of centre marker, sl 1-K1-psso, K2 tog, K to end.
Next row Cast (bind) off 5 sts, P to last 6 sts, (K1, P1) twice, K2.
Next row P2, (K1 tbl, P1) twice, K1 tbl, K to end.
Next row Cast (bind) off 5 sts, (one st on right-hand needle), P2 tog, P2 tog tbl, P to last 8 sts, P2 tog tbl, (K1, P1) twice, K2.
Next row P2, (K1 tbl, P1) twice, K1 tbl, K to end.
Next row Cast (bind) off the first 5 sts, then P to the last 6 sts, (K1,

P1) twice, K2. 14 sts rem.
Cast (bind) off in patt.

BUTTON BAND
Join raglan seams, ensuring that coloured-thread markers at beg of neck shaping on Sleeves are matched to end of cast- (bound-) off row at top of Right and Left Fronts.
Using smaller needles, cast on 13 sts.
1st rib row (RS) P1, *K1 tbl, P1, rep from * to end.
2nd rib row K1, *P1, K1, rep from * to end.
Rep last 2 rows until Band, slightly stretched, fits up Left Front and across top of Left Sleeve to centre back neck.
Cast (bind) off.
Sew Button Band to centre front edge of Left Front and across top of Left Sleeve to centre back neck.
Mark positions for 5 buttons on Button Band; the first 3cm (1¼") from cast-on edge, the top one at beg of V-neck shaping, and the others evenly spaced between.

BUTTONHOLE BAND
Work as for Button Band, making buttonholes to correspond with markers as foll:
1st buttonhole row (RS) Rib 5, cast (bind) off 3 sts, rib to end.
2nd buttonhole row Rib 5, cast on 3 sts, rib to end.

FINISHING
Press pieces lightly on WS following instructions on yarn label and omitting ribbing.
Sew Buttonhole Band to centre front edge of Right Front and across top of Right Sleeve to centre back neck. Join centre back seam.
Join side and sleeve seams.
Sew on buttons to correspond to buttonholes.
Press seams lightly on the WS following the instructions on the yarn label.

CHILLI SKIRT

ROWAN SILKSTONES

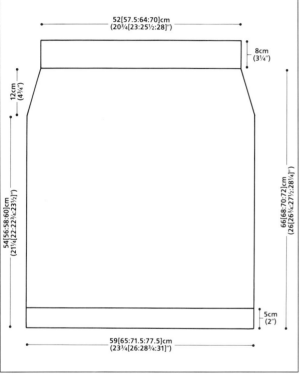

52[57.5:64:70]cm
(20¾[23:25½:28]")

8cm
(3¼")

12cm
(4¾")

66[68:70:72]cm
(26[26¾:27½:28¼]")

54[56:58:60]cm
(21¼[22:22¾:23½]")

5cm
(2")

59[65:71.5:77.5]cm
(23¾[26:28¾:31]")

SIZES
To fit 115[127:140:152]cm
(45[50:55:60]") hips closely
Finished measurement around
hips 118[130:143:155]cm
(47½[52:57½:62]")

Figures for larger sizes are given
in brackets; where there is only
one set of figures, it applies to all
sizes.
*See diagram for finished
measurements of back and front
skirt. Lengthen or shorten skirt at
position indicated in instructions.*

MATERIALS
7[8:10:11] x 50g (1¾oz) balls of
Rowan *Silkstones* in Chilli (shade
no. 826)
One pair each 3¼mm (US size 3)
and 4mm (US size 6) needles *or
size to obtain correct tension
(gauge)*
Waist-length piece of 3cm (1¼")
wide elastic

TENSION (GAUGE)
24 sts and 28 rows to 10cm (4")
over st st on 4mm (US size 6)
needles
*Check your tension (gauge)
before beginning.*

BACK
Using smaller needles, cast on
142[156:172:186] sts.
Work 5cm (2") in K1, P1 rib.
Change to larger needles and
beg with a K row, work in st st

until Skirt measures 54[56:58:
60]cm (21¼[22:22¾:23½]")
from beg *or* until it measures
12cm (4¾") less than the final
desired length (lengthen or
shorten here if desired), ending
with a WS row.
Dec one st at each end of next
and every foll 4th row until there
are 124[138:154:168] sts.
Work one row, so ending with a
P row.
Change to smaller needles and
work 8cm (3¼") in K1, P1 rib for
waistband.
Cast (bind) off in rib.

FRONT
Work as for Back.

FINISHING
Press pieces lightly on WS
following instructions on yarn
label and omitting ribbing.
Join side seams. Cut elastic to the
correct length allowing for
seams. Join ends of elastic. Fold
waist ribbing in half to WS
enclosing elastic and sew in
place.
Press seams lightly on the WS
following the instructions on the
yarn label.

CHILLI SWEATER

ROWAN SILKSTONES

SIZES
To choose appropriate size see
page 118
Finished measurement around
bust 110[120:130:140]cm
(44[48:52:56]")
Figures for larger sizes are given
in brackets; where there is only

one set of figures, it applies to all
sizes.
*See diagram for finished
measurements of back, front and
sleeves.*
*To lengthen or shorten the back
and the front, or the sleeves see
page 118.*

MATERIALS
8[9:10:11] x 50g (1¾oz) balls of
Rowan *Silkstones* in Chilli (shade
no. 826)
One pair each 3¼mm (US size 3)
and 4mm (US size 6) needles *or
size to obtain correct tension
(gauge)*

TENSION (GAUGE)
24 sts and 28 rows to 10cm (4")
over st st on 4mm (US size 6)
needles
*Check your tension (gauge)
before beginning.*

BACK

Using smaller needles, cast on 132[144:156:168] sts.
Work 10cm (4") in K1, P1 rib.**
Change to larger needles and beg with a K row, work in st st until Back measures 72[74:76:78]cm (28¼[29:29¾:30½]") from beg, ending with a WS row.
Cast (bind) off 39[44:49:54] sts at beg of next 2 rows.
Slip rem 54[56:58:60] sts onto a st holder for back neck.

FRONT

Work as for Back to **.
Change to larger needles and beg with a K row, work in st st until Front measures 64[66:68:70]cm (25[25¾:26½:27¼]") from beg, ending with a WS row.
Shape Neck
Next row (RS) K59[64:69:74], leaving rem sts on spare needle.
Working on first side of neck only and cont in st st throughout, cast (bind) off 3 sts at beg of next row (neck edge), then cast (bind) off at neck edge 3 sts on 2 foll alt rows and 2 sts on 2 foll alt rows. 46[51:56:61] sts.
Dec one st at neck edge on next and every foll row 7 times in all. 39[44:49:54] sts.
Work without shaping until there are same number of rows as Back to shoulder. Cast (bind) off.
Return to rem sts and with RS facing, slip centre 14[16:18:20] sts onto a st holder, rejoin yarn to rem sts and K across row.
Complete 2nd side of neck to match first side, reversing all shaping.

SLEEVES

Using smaller needles, cast on 48[50:52:54] sts.
Work 10cm (4") in K1, P1 rib.
Change to larger needles and beg with a K row, work in st st, inc one st at each end of next and every foll alt row 4[10:16:22] times in all. 56[70:84:98] sts.
Cont in st st throughout, work 2 rows without shaping.

Inc one st at each end of next and every foll 3rd row 26[21:16:11] times in all. 108[112:116:120] sts.
Work without shaping until Sleeve measures 46[45:44:43]cm (18[17¾:17¼:17]") from beg, ending with a WS row.
Cast (bind) off all sts.
Make 2nd Sleeve in same way.

NECKBAND

Press pieces as for Skirt.
Join right shoulder seam.
Using smaller needles and with RS facing, pick up and K24 sts down left front neck, K14[16:18:20] sts from st holder, pick up and K24 sts up right front neck and K54[56:58:60] sts from back neck st holder. 116[120:124:128] sts.
Work 5cm (2") in K1, P1 rib.
Cast (bind) off in rib.
Join left shoulder seam and neckband.
Fold Neckband in half to WS and sew in place.

COLLAR

Using smaller needles, cast on 12 sts. Work in st st for 86cm (34").
Do not break off yarn and slip sts onto a safety-pin.
Make a 2nd strip in same way.
Allow strips to form into rolls.
Pin cast-on edge of each strip to centre back neck. Twist strips around each other to form a braid 3.5cm (1⅜") wide and pin braid to neckband. Adjust length until braid fits to centre back neck. Cast (bind) off strips. Sew cast- (bound-) off edges of strips to cast-on edges at centre back neck. Sew braid carefully in place along neckband, securing at each crossing.

Finishing

Place markers on Back and Front 22.5[23:24:25]cm (9[9¼:9¾:10]") from shoulder seam.
Sew Sleeves to Back and Front between markers.
Join side and sleeve seams.
Press seams as for Skirt.

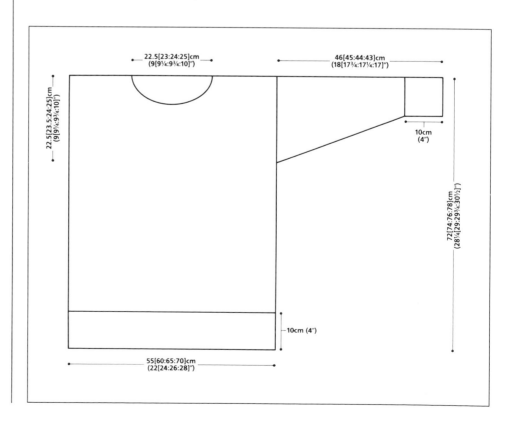

Dress up your Chilli collection with this wool and silk shawl or wear it as an evening wrap.

'Now, if this isn't sophisticated, the Pope doesn't pray.'

PAISLEY SHAWL
R O W A N S I L K S T O N E S

SIZE
62cm (24¾") wide by 180cm
(71") long

MATERIALS
Rowan *Silkstones*
7 x 50g (1¾oz) balls in Eau de Nil
(shade no. 835) A
2 x 50g (1¾oz) balls each in Chilli
(shade no. 826) B, Blue Mist
(shade no. 832) C and Natural
(shade no. 837) D
One pair 4mm (US size 6) needles
*or size to obtain correct tension
(gauge)*

TENSION (GAUGE)
24 sts and 29 rows to 10cm (4")
over st st on 4mm (US size 6)
needles
24 sts and 24 rows to 10cm (4")
over colour patt on 4mm (US size
6) needles
*Check your tension (gauge)
before beginning.*

NOTES
*When using more than one
colour in a row, carry colours not
in use loosely across back of
work, weaving around working
yarn to avoid long loose strands.
Read chart from right to left for
RS (knit) rows and from left to
right for WS (purl) rows.*

TO MAKE
Using 4mm (US size 6) needles
and yarn A, cast on 148 sts.
Beg moss (seed) st as foll:
1st moss (seed) st row (RS) *K1,
P1, rep from * to end.
2nd moss (seed) st row *P1,
K1, rep from * to end.
Rep last 2 rows to form moss
(seed) st.
Work in moss (seed) st until
shawl measures 5cm (2") from
beg, ending with a WS row.

PAISLEY CHART

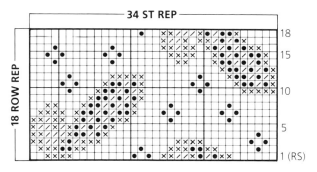

COLOUR KEY
□ = A (Eau de Nil)
▣ = B (Chilli)
☒ = C (Blue Mist)
☑ = D (Natural)

Beg paisley colour patt on next
row as foll:
1st patt row (RS) Using yarn A
(K1, P1) 3 times, K next 136 sts in
colour patt foll first chart row
(see *Notes* above) and rep 34-st
rep 4 times in all across these 136
sts, then using yarn A (K1, P1) 3
times.
Cont in this way, keeping first 6
and last 6 sts in moss (seed) st
and working in st st foll chart for
colour patt until all 18 rows of
chart have been completed.
Then cont in patt as set, rep the
18 rows of the chart until chart
has been rep 4 times in all from
beg (72 colour patt rows in all),

so ending with a WS row.
Using yarn A only and beg with a
K row, work in st st, keeping first
6 and last 6 sts in moss (seed) st
throughout, until shawl measures
145cm (57") from beg, ending
with a WS row.
Beg with first chart row, work 18-
row rep of chart 4 times (72
rows) as before.
Using yarn A, work 5cm (2") in
moss (seed) st.
Cast (bind) off all sts.

FINISHING
Press lightly on WS following
instructions on yarn label and
omitting moss (seed) st.

BORDER JACKET

ROWANFLECK DK

SIZES
To choose appropriate size see page 118
Finished measurement around bust 116[126:137:146]cm (46½[50½:54½:58½]")
Figures for larger sizes are given in brackets; where there is only one set of figures, it applies to all sizes.
See diagram for finished measurements of back, fronts and sleeves. To lengthen or shorten back and fronts, or sleeves see page 118.

MATERIALS
11[12:13:14] x 50g (1¾oz) balls of *Rowan Rowanfleck* DK in main colour – Sienna (shade no. 77F) A
Rowan *Designer DK* in the foll 5 contrasting colours:
4[5:5:6] x 50g (1¾oz) balls in Red (shade no. 640) B
2[2:2:3] x 50g (1¾oz) ball each in Copper (shade no. 627) C
1 x 50g (1¾oz) ball each in Gold (shade no. 641) D, Aqua (shade no. 89) E and Dark Green (shade no. 655) F
One pair each 3¼mm (US size 3) and 4mm (US size 6) needles *or size to obtain correct tension (gauge)*
Eight 1.5cm (⅝") buttons

TENSION (GAUGE)
24 sts and 24 rows to 10cm (4") over chart 2 colour patt on 4mm (US size 6) needles
23 sts and 28 rows to 10cm (4") over st st on 4mm (US size 6) needles and using yarn A
Check your tension (gauge) before beginning.

NOTES
When using only 2 colours in a row, carry the yarn not in use loosely across back of work. When working rows 6-23 of chart 3, do not strand yarns across back of work, but use a separate ball of yarn for each isolated area of colour, twisting yarns at back when changing colours to avoid holes.
Read charts from right to left for RS (knit) rows and from left to right for WS (purl) rows.

BACK
Using smaller needles and yarn B, cast on 134[146:160:170] sts.
Work one row in K1, P1 rib.
Change to yarn A and cont in rib until ribbing measures 9cm (3½") from beg, inc one st at end of last row for first, 2nd and 4th sizes only. 135[147:160:171] sts.
**Change to larger needles and beg with a K row, work 2 rows in st st.
Beg with first chart row (K row), work in st st foll chart 1 (see *Notes* above) as indicated for chosen size until all 4 chart rows have been completed.
Beg with first chart row (K row), work in st st foll chart 2 beg and ending as indicated for your chosen size until all of the 8 chart rows have been completed.
Cont rep 8 chart rows of chart 2 until Back of jacket measures 41[43:45:47]cm (16¼[17:17¾: 18½]") from beg, ending with a WS row.
Beg with first chart row (K row), work in st st foll chart 3 as indicated for chosen size until all 28 chart rows have been completed, so ending with a WS

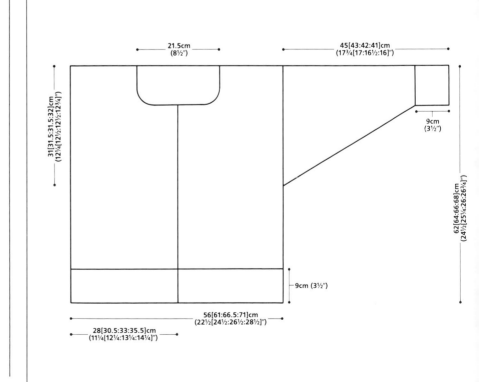

A boxy jacket with a floral pattern across the front and back, and a matching skirt. If you prefer a longer length jacket it can be easily adjusted to the length you want (see page 118).

'Stunning and not too "girlie".'

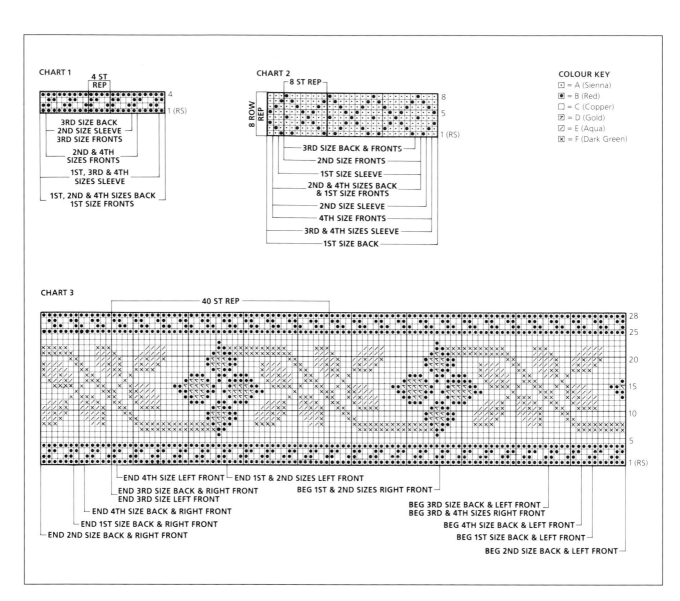

CHART 1

4 ST REP

4

1 (RS)

3RD SIZE BACK
2ND SIZE SLEEVE
3RD SIZE FRONTS

2ND & 4TH
SIZES FRONTS

1ST, 3RD & 4TH
SIZES SLEEVE

1ST, 2ND & 4TH SIZES BACK
1ST SIZE FRONTS

CHART 2

8 ST REP

8 ROW REP

8

5

1 (RS)

3RD SIZE BACK & FRONTS
2ND SIZE FRONTS
1ST SIZE SLEEVE
2ND & 4TH SIZES BACK
& 1ST SIZE FRONTS
2ND SIZE SLEEVE
4TH SIZE FRONTS
3RD & 4TH SIZES SLEEVE
1ST SIZE BACK

COLOUR KEY

· = A (Sienna)
● = B (Red)
□ = C (Copper)
▨ = D (Gold)
▨ = E (Aqua)
☒ = F (Dark Green)

CHART 3

40 ST REP

28
25
20
15
10
5
1 (RS)

END 4TH SIZE LEFT FRONT
END 3RD SIZE BACK & RIGHT FRONT
END 3RD SIZE LEFT FRONT
END 4TH SIZE BACK & RIGHT FRONT
END 1ST SIZE BACK & RIGHT FRONT
END 2ND SIZE BACK & RIGHT FRONT

END 1ST & 2ND SIZES LEFT FRONT
BEG 1ST & 2ND SIZES RIGHT FRONT

BEG 3RD SIZE BACK & LEFT FRONT
BEG 3RD & 4TH SIZES RIGHT FRONT
BEG 4TH SIZE BACK & LEFT FRONT
BEG 1ST SIZE BACK & LEFT FRONT
BEG 2ND SIZE BACK & LEFT FRONT

row.** This completes chart patts. Using yarn A, dec 6 sts across next row as foll:
Next row (RS) (K2 tog, K25[27: 30:32]) 4 times, K2 tog, K23[27: 28:31], K2 tog. 129[141:154: 165] sts.
Using yarn A, cont in st st without shaping until Back measures 62[64:66:68]cm (24½[25¼:26:26¾]") from beg, ending with a WS row.
Cast (bind) off 40[46:53:58] sts at beg of next 2 rows.
Slip rem 49[49:48:49] sts onto a st holder for back neck.

LEFT FRONT
Using smaller needles and yarn B, cast on 66[72:80:84] sts.

Work one row in K1, P1 rib. Change to yarn A and cont in rib until ribbing measures 9cm (3½") from beg, inc one st at end of last row for first, 2nd and 4th sizes only. 67[73:80:85] sts.
Work as for Back from ** to **.
Shape Neck
Using yarn A, beg shaping neck on next row as foll:***
Next row (RS) K2 tog, K25[27: 30:32], K2 tog, K23[27:31:34], turn leaving rem 15 sts on a st holder.
Cont in st st on these 50[56: 63:68] sts, cast (bind) off 2 sts at beg of next row and at beg of every foll alt row 3 times in all, then dec one st at neck edge on every foll alt row 4 times.

40[46:53:58] sts.
Work in st st without shaping until there are same number of rows as Back to shoulder, ending with a WS row.
Cast (bind) off all sts.

RIGHT FRONT
Work as for Left Front to ***. Break off yarn.
Next row (RS) Slip first 15 sts onto a st holder, rejoin yarn A and K23[27:31:34], K2 tog, K to last 2 sts, K2 tog. 50[56:63:68] sts.
Complete as for Left Front, reversing all shaping.

SLEEVES
Using smaller needles and yarn B,

cast on 54[56:58:58] sts.
Work one row in K1, P1 rib.
Change to yarn A and cont in rib until cuff measures 9cm (3½") from beg.
Next row (inc row) Rib 1[2:3:3], *work into front and back of next st – called inc 1 –*, [then (rib 2, inc 1 in next st) twice, rib 1, inc 1 in next st] 6 times, rib 2, inc 1 in next st, rib 1[2:3:3]. 74[76:78:78] sts.
Change to larger needles and beg with a K row, work 2 rows in st st, inc one st at each end of every row. 78[80:82:82] sts.
Beg with first chart row (K row), work in st st foll chart 1 as indicated for chosen size until all 4 chart rows have been completed *and at the same time* shape Sleeve by inc one st at each end of next and every foll alt row. 82[84:86:86] sts.
Work first chart row of chart 2 as indicated for chosen size.
Cont foll chart 2 until all 8 chart rows have been completed, then cont rep 8 chart rows *and at the same time* cont shaping Sleeve by inc one st at each end of next and every foll alt row until there are 148[150:152:154] sts, keeping patt correct throughout.
Cont in patt without shaping until the Sleeve measures 45[43:42:41]cm (17¾[17:16½:16]") from beg, ending with a WS row.
Cast (bind) off all sts.
Make 2nd Sleeve in the same way.

BUTTON BAND
Join shoulder seams.
Using smaller needles and yarn B, cast on 11 sts.
1st rib row (RS) K1, *P1, K1, rep from * to end.
Change to yarn A.
2nd rib row P1, *K1, P1, rep from * to end.
Using yarn A only, rep last 2 rows until Band, slightly stretched, fits up Front to beg of neck shaping, ending with a 2nd rib row.

Break off yarn and leave sts on a safety-pin.
Sew Button Band to centre front edge of Left Front.
Mark positions for 7 buttons on Button Band; the first 1.5cm (½") from cast-on edge and the others evenly spaced between first and safety-pin.

BUTTONHOLE BAND
Work as for Button Band, but do not break off yarn and make buttonholes to correspond with markers as foll:
1st buttonhole row (RS) Rib 4, cast (bind) off 3 sts, rib to end.
2nd buttonhole row Rib 4, cast on 3 sts, rib to end.
Sew Buttonhole Band to centre edge of Right Front.

NECKBAND
Using smaller needles and yarn A and with RS facing, rib across 11 sts of Buttonhole Band, then K15 sts from st holder, pick up and K15 sts up right front neck, K49[49:48:49] sts from back neck st holder, pick up and K15 sts down left front neck, K15 sts from st holder, then rib across 11 sts of Button Band.
Work one row in K1, P1 rib, inc one st along back neck of 3rd size only, so ending at right front edge. 131 sts.
1st buttonhole row (RS) Rib 4, cast (bind) off 3 sts, rib to end.
2nd buttonhole row (RS) Rib to last 7 sts, cast on 3 sts, rib to end.
Rib 3 rows.
Change to yarn B and rib one row.
Using yarn B, cast (bind) off in rib.

FINISHING
Press pieces lightly on WS with a warm iron over a damp cloth, omitting ribbing.
Place markers on Back and Fronts 31[31.5:31.5:32]cm (12¼[12½:12½:12¾]") from left and right shoulder seam.

Sew Sleeves to Back and Fronts between markers.
Join side and sleeve seams.
Sew on buttons to correspond to buttonholes.
Press seams lightly on WS with a warm iron over a damp cloth.

BORDER SKIRT

R O W A N F L E C K D K

SIZES

To fit 102[112:122:132]cm
(40[44:48:52]") hips closely
Finished measurement around
hips 104[115:125:136]cm
(42[46:50:54]")
Figures for larger sizes are given
in brackets; where there is only
one set of figures, it applies to all
sizes.
*See diagram for finished
measurements of back and front
skirt. Lengthen or shorten skirt at
position indicated in instructions.*

MATERIALS

9[10:11:12] x 50g (1¾oz) balls of
Rowan *Rowanfleck DK* in Sienna
(shade no. 77F) A
1 x 50g (1¾oz) ball of Rowan
Designer DK in Red (shade no.
640) B
One pair each 3¼mm (US size 3)
and 4mm (US size 6) needles *or
size to obtain correct tension
(gauge)*
Waist-length piece of 2.5cm (1")
wide elastic

TENSION (GAUGE)

23 sts and 28 rows to 10cm (4")
over st st on 4mm (US size 6)
needles and using yarn A
*Check your tension (gauge)
before beginning.*

NOTES

*When using 2 colours in a row,
carry the yarn not in use loosely
across back of work.
Read chart from right to left for
RS (knit) rows and from left to
right for WS (purl) rows.*

BACK

Using smaller needles and yarn B,
cast on 110[122:134:146] sts.
Work 8 rows in K1, P1 rib.
Change to larger needles and
yarn A, and beg with a K row,
work 2 rows in st st.
Beg with first chart row (K row),
work in st st foll skirt chart (see
Notes above) as indicated for
chosen size until all 4 chart rows
have been completed, so ending
with a WS row.
Using yarn A and beg with a K
row, work in st st inc one st at
each end of next and every foll
26th row 5 times in all. 120[132:
144:156] sts.
Cont in st st throughout, work
without shaping until Skirt
measures 64[66:68:70]cm
(25¼[26:26¾:27½]") from beg
or until it measures 12cm (4¾")
less than final desired length
(lengthen or shorten here),
ending with a WS row.
Dec one st at each end of next
and every foll 4th row until there
are 102[114:126:138] sts.
Work one row without shaping.
Change to smaller needles and
work 16 rows in K1, P1 rib for
waistband.
Cast (bind) off in rib.

FRONT

Work as for Back.

FINISHING

Press pieces lightly on WS with a
warm iron over a damp cloth,
omitting ribbing.
Join side seams. Cut elastic to the
correct length allowing for
seams. Join ends of elastic. Fold
waist ribbing in half to WS
enclosing elastic and sew in
place.
Press seams lightly on WS with a
warm iron over a damp cloth,
omitting ribbing.

44[49.5:55:60]cm
(17¾[19¾:22:24]")

6cm (2½")

12cm
(4¾")

76[78:80:82]cm
(30[30¾:31½:32¼]")

64[66:68:70]cm
(25¼[26:26¾:27½]")

52[57.5:62.5:68]cm
(21[23:25:27]")

SKIRT CHART

4 ST
REP

4

1 (RS)

2ND & 4TH SIZES

1ST & 3RD SIZES

COLOUR KEY
⊡ = A (Sienna)
◉ = B (Red)

FLORAL CARDIGAN

ROWAN MAGPIE ARAN

SIZE
One size only (see page 118 for choosing size)
Finished measurement around bust 156cm (61¾")
See diagram for finished measurements of back, fronts and sleeves. To lengthen or shorten back and fronts, or sleeves see page 118.

MATERIALS
Rowan *Magpie Aran*
11 x 100g (3½oz) hanks in Natural (shade no. 002) A
3 x 100g (3½oz) hanks in Raven (shade no. 62) B
One pair each 4mm (US size 6) and 5mm (US size 8) needles *or size to obtain correct tension (gauge)*
Five 2.5cm (1") buttons

TENSION (GAUGE)
18 sts and 23 rows to 10cm (4") over st st on 5mm (US size 8) needles
Check your tension (gauge) before beginning.

NOTES
Back and Fronts are worked from combined chart until chart row 124 has been completed. The combined chart then continues for Fronts only and Back continues on separate upper back chart.
When working colour patt do not strand yarn B across entire row at back of work, but strand it only across area it is used in, twisting yarns at back when changing colours to avoid holes; strand yarn A across entire row. When stranding, weave yarn not in use around working yarn.
Read the charts from right to left for RS (knit) rows and from left

to right for WS (purl) rows.

BACK
Using smaller needles and yarn A, cast on 136 sts.
Beg K2, P2 rib as foll:
1st rib row *K2, P2, rep from * to end.
Rep last row until rib measures 10cm (4") from beg.
Change to larger needles and beg with a first chart row (K row), work in st st foll chart for back/fronts (see *Notes* above) until 118th chart row has been completed, so ending with a WS row.

Shape Armholes
Cont to foll chart for colour patt throughout, cast (bind) off 12 sts at beg of next 2 rows. 112 sts.
Cont without shaping until 124th chart row has been completed,

then foll upper back chart from 125th row until 188th chart row has been completed, so ending with a WS row.

Shape Shoulders
Cast (bind) off 9 sts at beg of next 4 rows, then cast (bind) off 8 sts at beg of next 2 rows, and 7 sts at beg of foll 2 rows.
Cast (bind) off rem 46 sts for back neck.

LEFT FRONT
Using smaller needles and yarn A, cast on 68 sts.
Work 10cm (4") in K2, P2 rib as for Back.
Change to larger needles and beg with a first chart row (K row), work in st st foll chart, ending where indicated, until 99th row has been completed, so ending with a RS row.

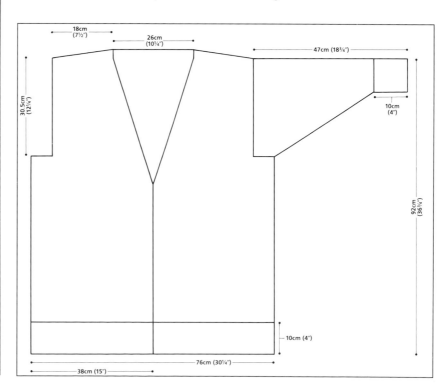

1 (RS)　10　20　30　40　50　60　70　80　90

UPPER BACK CHART

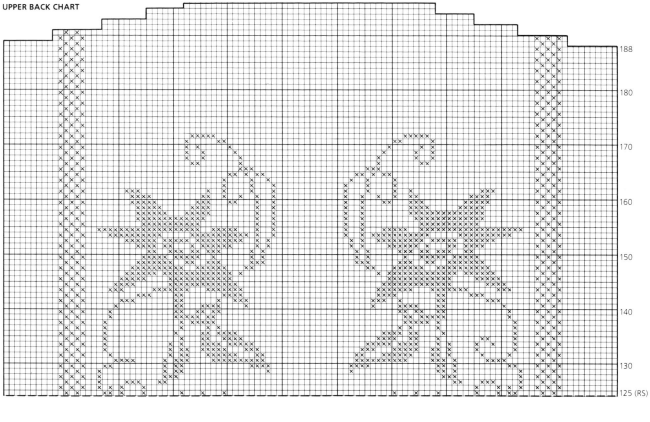

188
180
170
160
150
140
130
125 (RS)

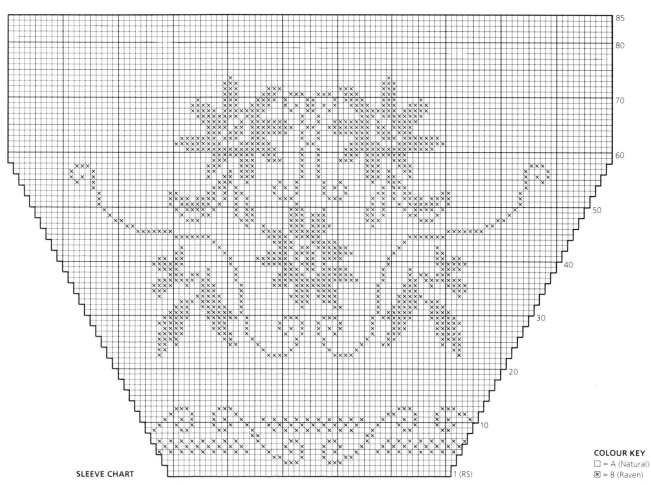

85
80
70
60
50
40
30
20
10
1 (RS)

SLEEVE CHART

COLOUR KEY
☐ = A (Natural)
☒ = B (Raven)

WINTER WARMERS

This chapter includes two of the most useful jackets you'll ever want to knit, plus five other gorgeous knits for those chilly winter days. Plain, patterned or chunky snuggle into these!

WINTER FAIRISLE

R O W A N S P U N   T W E E D

SIZES

To choose appropriate size see page 118
Finished measurement around bust 111[124:138:151]cm (44½[50:55:60½]")
Figures for larger sizes are given in brackets; where there is only one set of figures, it applies to all sizes.
See diagram for finished measurements of back, front and sleeves. To lengthen or shorten back and front, or sleeves see page 118.

MATERIALS

7[8:8:10] x 100g (3½oz) hanks of Rowan *Rowanspun Tweed* in main colour – One AM (shade no. 756) A
2[2:2:3] x 25g (1oz) hanks of Rowan *Botany* in each of 4 contrasting colours – Red (shade no. 45) B, Green (shade no. 91) C, Yellow (shade no. 629) D and Blue (shade no. 55) E
One pair each 4mm (US size 6) and 4½mm (US size 7) needles *or size to obtain correct tension (gauge)*

TENSION (GAUGE)

18 sts and 26 rows to 10cm (4") over st st on 4½mm (US size 7) needles
Check your tension (gauge) before beginning.

NOTES

Use yarns B, C, D and E double throughout.
When using 2 colours in a row, carry the yarn not in use loosely across the back of the work. Read charts from right to left for RS (knit) rows and from left to right for WS (purl) rows. Note that charts 1 and 3 beg with a WS row, and charts 3 and 4 beg with a RS row.

BACK

Using smaller needles and yarn A, cast on 101[113:125:137] sts.
Beg moss (seed) st as foll:
1st moss (seed) st row (RS) P1, *K1, P1, rep from * to end.
Rep last row to form moss (seed) st.
Work in moss (seed) st until Back measures 14cm (5½") from beg, dec one st at end of last row and ending with a RS row. 100[112: 124:136] sts.
Change to larger needles and (remembering to use yarn B double throughout) beg chart 1 (see *Notes* above) as foll:
1st row (WS) P3[1:3:1]A, 2B, 1A, 2B, *3A, 2B, 1A, 2B, rep from *

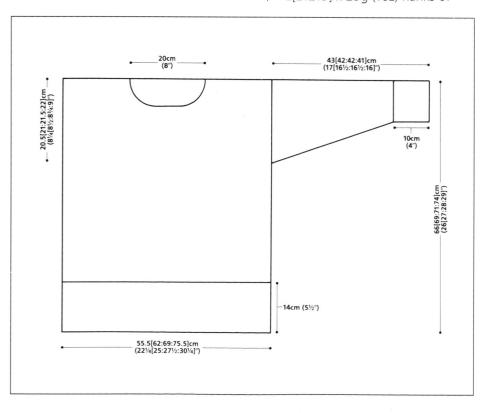

20cm
(8")

43[42:42:41]cm
(17[16½:16½:16]")

10cm
(4")

20.5[21:21.5:22]cm
(8¼[8¼:8½:8¾]")

66[69:71:74]cm
(26[27:28:29]")

14cm (5½")

55.5[62:69:75.5]cm
(22¼[25:27½:30¼]")

An updated interpretation of a traditional design, bright contrasts knitted into a rich navy flecked background.

'Busy but not gauche, I call this. You can almost smell the heather.'

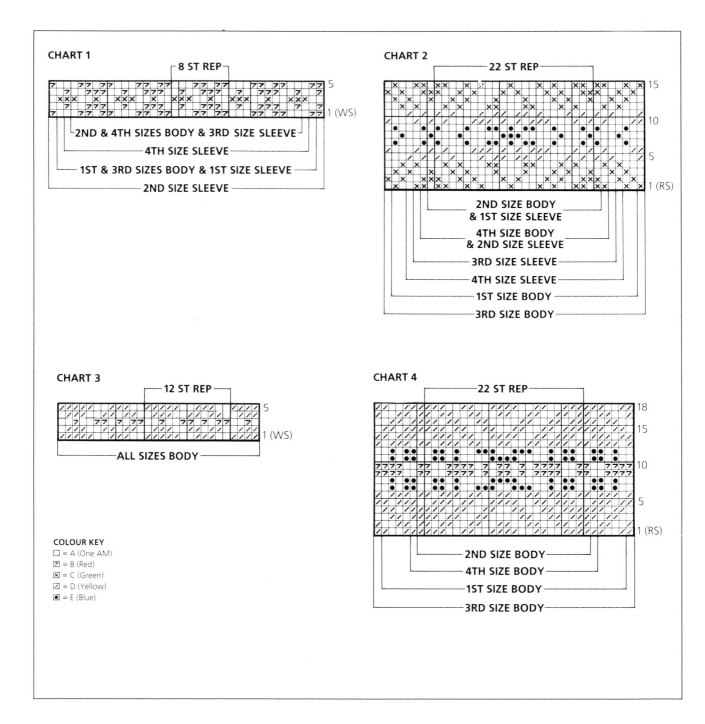

CHART 1

8 ST REP

5
1 (WS)

2ND & 4TH SIZES BODY & 3RD SIZE SLEEVE
4TH SIZE SLEEVE
1ST & 3RD SIZES BODY & 1ST SIZE SLEEVE
2ND SIZE SLEEVE

CHART 2

22 ST REP

15
10
5
1 (RS)

2ND SIZE BODY
& 1ST SIZE SLEEVE
4TH SIZE BODY
& 2ND SIZE SLEEVE
3RD SIZE SLEEVE
4TH SIZE SLEEVE
1ST SIZE BODY
3RD SIZE BODY

CHART 3

12 ST REP

5
1 (WS)

ALL SIZES BODY

COLOUR KEY
☐ = A (One AM)
☑ = B (Red)
☒ = C (Green)
☑ = D (Yellow)
◉ = E (Blue)

CHART 4

22 ST REP

18
15
10
5
1 (RS)

2ND SIZE BODY
4TH SIZE BODY
1ST SIZE BODY
3RD SIZE BODY

to last 4[2:4:2] sts, ending with 3[2:3:2]A, 1[0:1:0]B.
2nd row K2[0:2:0]A, *1B, 2A, 3B, 2A, rep from * to last 2[0:2:0] sts, ending with 1[0:1:0]B, 1[0:1:0]A.
The first 2 rows of patt are now set.
Beg with 3rd chart row (P row),

cont in st st foll chart 1 until all 5 rows of chart have been completed, so ending with a P row.
Using yarn A only and beg with a K row, work 2 rows in st st.
First size only:
Beg chart 2 as foll:
1st row (RS) K1A, 1C, 2A, 2C,

*1A, 2C, 2A, 1C, 1A, (1C, 3A) twice, 1C, 1A, 1C, 2A, 2C, rep from * to last 6 sts, ending with 1A, 2C, 2A, 1C.
2nd row P1A, 1C, 2A, 3C, *2A, (1C, 1A, 1C, 3A) twice, 1C, 1A, 1C, 2A, 3C, rep from * to last 5 sts, ending with 2A, 1C, 1A, 1C.
2nd size only:

Beg chart 2 as foll:
1st row (RS) K1C, *1A, 2C, 2A, 1C, 1A, (1C, 3A) twice, 1C, 1A, 1C, 2A, 2C, rep from * to last st, ending with 1A.
2nd row P2C, *2A, (1C, 1A, 1C, 3A) twice, 1C, 1A, 1C, 2A, 3C, rep from * to end.
3rd size only:
Beg chart 2 as foll:
1st row (RS) K1C, 1A, 1C, 2A, 2C, *1A, 2C, 2A, 1C, 1A, (1C, 3A) twice, 1C, 1A, 1C, 2A, 2C, rep from * to last 6 sts, ending with 1A, 2C, 2A, 1C, 1A.
2nd row P1C, 1A, 1C, 2A, 3C, *2A, (1C, 1A, 1C, 3A) twice, 1C, 1A, 1C, 2A, 3C, rep from * to last 6 sts, ending with 2A, (1C, 1A) twice.
4th size only:
Beg chart 2 as foll:
1st row (RS) K2C, *1A, 2C, 2A, 1C, 1A, (1C, 3A) twice, 1C, 1A, 1C, 2A, 2C, rep from * to last 2 sts, ending with 1A, 1C.
2nd row P3C, *2A, (1C, 1A, 1C, 3A) twice, 1C, 1A, 1C, 2A, 3C, rep from * to last st, ending with 1A.
All sizes:
The first 2 rows of patt are now set. Beg with 3rd chart row (K row), cont in st st foll chart 2 until all 15 rows of chart have been completed, so ending with a K row.
Using yarn A only and beg with a P row, work 3[5:6:7]cm (1¼[2: 2¼:2¾]”) in st st, ending with a K row.
Beg chart 3 as foll:
1st row (WS) *P5D, 2A, 3D, 2A, rep from * to last 4 sts, ending with 4D.
2nd row *K3D, 2A, 2D, 1A, 2D, 2A, rep from * to last 4 sts, ending with 3D, 1A.
The first 2 rows of patt are now set. Beg with 3rd chart row (P row), cont in st st foll chart 3 until all 5 rows of chart have been completed, so ending with a P row.
Using yarn A only and beg with a K row, work 7[8:9:11]cm (2¾

[3:3½:4½]”) in st st, ending with a K row.
Work 5 rows of chart 1, working first and 2nd rows as before.
Using yarn A only and beg with a K row, work 2 rows in st st.
Work 15 rows of chart 2 as before.
Using yarn A only and beg with a P row, work in st st until Back measures 55[58:60:63]cm (21¾ [22¾:23¾:24¾]”) from beg, ending with a K row.
Work 5 rows of chart 3 as before.
Using yarn A only and beg with a K row, work 2 rows in st st, so ending with a P row.**
First size only:
Beg chart 4 as foll:
1st row (RS) K1D, 2A, 6D, *2A, 2D, 2A, 4D, 2A, 2D, 2A, 6D, rep from * to last 3 sts, ending with 2A, 1D.
2nd row P2A, (2D, 1A) twice, *(2D, 2A) 4 times, (2D, 1A) twice, rep from * to last 4 sts, ending with 2D, 2A.
2nd size only:
Beg chart 4 as foll:
1st row (RS) K4D, *2A, 2D, 2A, 4D, 2A, 2D, 2A, 6D, rep from *, ending last rep with 4D instead of 6D.
2nd row *P2D, 1A, (2D, 2A) 4 times, 2D, 1A, rep from * to last 2 sts, ending with 2D.
3rd size only:
Beg chart 4 as foll:
1st row (RS) K2D, 2A, 6D, *2A, 2D, 2A, 4D, 2A, 2D, 2A, 6D, rep from * to last 4 sts, ending with 2A, 2D.
2nd row P1D, 2A, (2D, 1A) twice, *(2D, 2A) 4 times, (2D, 1A) twice, rep from * to last 5 sts, ending with 2D, 2A, 1D.
4th size only:
Beg chart 4 as foll:
1st row (RS) K5D, *2A, 2D, 2A, 4D, 2A, 2D, 2A, 6D, rep from *, ending last rep with 5D instead of 6D.
2nd row P1A, *2D, 1A, (2D, 2A) 4 times, 2D, 1A, rep from * to last 3 sts, ending with 2D, 1A.

All sizes:
The first 2 rows of patt are now set. Beg with 3rd chart row (K row), cont in st st foll chart 4 until all 18 rows of chart have been completed, so ending with a P row.
Using yarn A only and beg with a K row, work 2 rows in st st.
Cast (bind) off 32[38:44:50] sts at beg of next 2 rows.
Slip rem 36 sts onto a st holder for back neck.

FRONT
Work as for Back to **.
Shape Neck
Beg chart 4 as for Back *and at the same time* shape neck as foll:
Next row (RS) Work 40[46:52: 58] sts in patt, turn leaving rem sts on a spare needle.
Keeping patt correct throughout and working on first side of neck only, dec one st at neck edge on every row 4 times. 36[42:48:54] sts.
Work one row in patt without shaping.
Dec one st at neck edge on next and every foll alt row 4 times in all. 32[38:44:50] sts.
Work without shaping until all 18 rows of chart 4 have been completed, so ending with a P row.
Then using yarn A only and beg with a K row, work 2 rows in st st.
Cast (bind) off.
Return to rem sts and with RS facing, slip centre 20 sts onto a st holder, rejoin yarn to rem sts and work across row in patt.
Complete 2nd side of neck to match first side, reversing all shaping.

SLEEVES
Using smaller needles and yarn B, cast on 44[46:48:50] sts.
Using yarn A, work in K1, P1 rib for 10cm (4”).
Change to larger needles and beg with a K row, work 3 rows in st st.

Beg chart 1 as foll:
1st row (WS) P0[1:0:0]B, 3[3:
1:2]A, 2B, 1A, 2B, *3A, 2B, 1A,
2B, rep from * to last 4[5:2:3]
sts, ending with 3[3:2:3]A, 1[2:
0:0]B.
2nd row K0[1:0:0]B, 2[2:0:1]A,
*1B, 2A, 3B, 2A, rep from * to
last 2[3:0:1] sts, ending with
1[1:0:1]B, 1[2:0:0]A.
The first 2 rows of patt are now
set.
Beg with 3rd chart row (P row),
cont in st st foll chart 1 until all 5
rows of chart have been
completed, so ending with a P
row.
Using yarn A only and beg with a
K row, work 2 rows in st st, inc
one st at each end of last row.
46[48:50:52] sts.
First size only:
Beg chart 2 as foll:
1st row (RS) K1C, *1A, 2C, 2A,
1C, 1A, (1C, 3A) twice, 1C, 1A,
1C, 2A, 2C, rep from * to last st,
ending with 1A.
2nd row P2C, *2A, (1C, 1A, 1C,
3A) twice, 1C, 1A, 1C, 2A, 3C,
rep from * to end.
2nd size only:
1st row (RS) K2C, *1A, 2C, 2A,
1C, 1A, (1C, 3A) twice, 1C, 1A,
1C, 2A, 2C, rep from * to last 2
sts, ending with 1A, 1C.
2nd row P3C, *2A, (1C, 1A, 1C,
3A) twice, 1C, 1A, 1C, 2A, 3C,
rep from * to last st, ending with
1A.
3rd size only:
Beg chart 2 as foll:
1st row (RS) K1A, 2C, *1A, 2C,
2A, 1C, 1A, (1C, 3A) twice, 1C,
1A, 1C, 2A, 2C, rep from * to last
3 sts, ending with 1A, 2C.
2nd row P1A, 3C, *2A, (1C, 1A,
1C, 3A) twice, 1C, 1A, 1C, 2A,
3C, rep from * to last 2 sts,
ending with 2A.
4th size only:
Beg chart 2 on next row as foll:
1st row (RS) K2A, 2C, *1A, 2C,
2A, 1C, 1A, (1C, 3A) twice, 1C,
1A, 1C, 2A, 2C, rep from * to last
4 sts, ending with 1A, 2C, 1A.
2nd row P2A, 3C, *2A, (1C, 1A,

1C, 3A) twice, 1C, 1A, 1C, 2A,
3C, rep from * to last 3 sts,
ending with 2A, 1C.
All sizes:
The first 2 rows of patt are now
set. Beg with 3rd chart row (K
row), cont in st st foll chart 2
until all 15 rows of chart have
been completed, then beg with a
P row and using yarn A only,
cont in st st *and at the same time*
cont to shape Sleeve by inc one
st at each end of 4th, 8th and
12th chart rows and then every
4th foll row until there are
74[76:78:80] sts.
Cont in st st without shaping
until Sleeve measures 43[42:42:
41]cm (17[16½:16½:16]″) from
beg.
Cast (bind) off all sts.
Make 2nd Sleeve in the same
way.

COLLAR

Join the right shoulder seam.
Using smaller needles and yarn A
and with RS facing, pick up and
K17 sts down left front neck, K20
from st holder, pick up and K17
sts up right front neck and K36
sts from back neck st holder.
90 sts.
Using yarn B, P one row and K
one row.
Using yarn A, work in K1, P1 rib
for 4cm (1½″).
Using B, rib one row and then
cast (bind) off in rib.

FINISHING

Press pieces lightly on WS with a
warm iron over a damp cloth,
omitting the ribbing and moss
(seed) st.
Join left shoulder seam and collar
using backstitch.
Place markers on Back and Front
20.5[21:21.5:22]cm (8¼[8½:
8¾:9]″) from shoulder seam.
Sew Sleeves to Back and Front
between markers using
backstitch.
Join side and sleeve seams.
Press seams lightly on WS with a
warm iron over a damp cloth.

FIREFLY, NELSON AND NAUTILUS

ROWAN BRIGHT TWEED

SIZES

To choose appropriate size see page 118
Finished measurement around bust 126[138:150]cm (50[55½: 60]")
Figures for larger sizes are given in brackets; where there is only one set of figures, it applies to all sizes.
See diagram for finished measurements of back, front and sleeves. To lengthen or shorten back and front, or sleeves see page 118.

12[13:13] x 100g (3½oz) hanks of Rowan *Bright Tweed* in Nelson (shade no. 723)
Set of four 4½mm (US size 7) double-pointed needles (or short circular needle of same size)
For the Nautilus version only:
12[13:13] x 100g (3½oz) hanks of Rowan *Bright Tweed* in Nautilus (shade no. 727)
All versions:
One pair each 4½mm (US size 7) and 5½mm (US size 9) needles *or size to obtain correct tension (gauge)*

NOTES

The three versions of this sweater are worked in different colours, but they are made in exactly the same way except when working neckband or collar.

BACK

Using smaller needles, cast on 94[104:112] sts.
Work 11cm (4¼") in K1, P1 rib.**
Change to larger needles and beg with a K row, work in st st until Back measures 74[78:82]cm (29[30½:32]" from beg, ending with a WS row.
Cast (bind) off 32[36:39] sts at beg of next 2 rows.
Slip rem 30[32:34] sts onto a st holder for back neck.

FRONT

Work as for Back to **.
Change to larger needles and beg with a K row, work in st st until Front measures 66[70: 74]cm (26[27½:29]") from beg, ending with a WS row.
Shape Neck
Beg neck shaping on next row as foll:
Next row (RS) K37[41:44], turn leaving rem sts on a spare needle.
Working on first side of neck only and cont in st st throughout, dec one st at neck edge on next and every foll alt row 5 times in all. 32[36:39] sts.
Work without shaping until there are same number of rows as Back to shoulder.
Cast (bind) off.
Return to rem sts and with RS facing, slip centre 20[22:24] sts onto a st holder, rejoin yarn to rem sts and K across row.
Complete the 2nd side of the neck to match the first side,

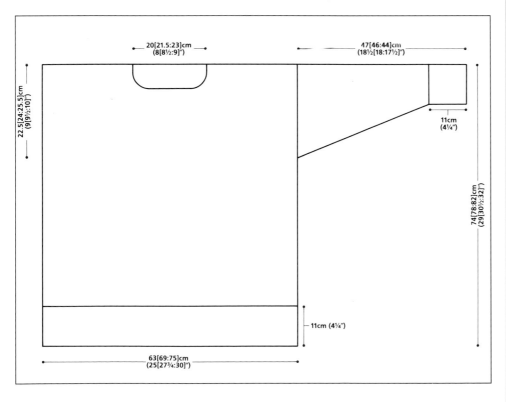

20[21.5:23]cm
(8[8½:9]")

47[46:44]cm
(18½[18:17½]")

22.5[24:25.5]cm
(9[9½:10]")

11cm
(4¼")

74[78:82]cm
(29[30½:32]")

11cm (4¼")

63[69:75]cm
(25[27¾:30]")

MATERIALS

For the Firefly version only:
12[13:13] x 100g (3½oz) hanks of Rowan *Bright Tweed* in Firefly (shade no. 720)
For the Nelson version only:

TENSION (GAUGE)

15 sts and 22 rows to 10cm (4") over st st on 5½mm (US size 9) needles
Check your tension (gauge) before beginning.

reversing all of the shaping.

SLEEVES
Using smaller needles, cast on 40[44:48] sts.
Work 11cm (4¼") in K1, P1 rib.
Change to larger needles and beg with a K row, work in st st, inc one st at each end of next and every foll 5th row until there are 68[72:76] sts.
Cont in st st without shaping until Sleeve measures 47[46:44]cm (18½[18:17½]") from beg, ending with a WS row.
Cast (bind) off all sts.
Make 2nd Sleeve in the same way.

FIREFLY NECKBAND
Press pieces on WS with a warm iron over a damp cloth, omitting ribbing.
Join right shoulder seam.
Work the Neckband, for the Firefly version only, as foll:
Using smaller needles and with RS facing, pick up and K16 sts down left front neck, K20[22:24] sts from st holder, pick up and K16 sts up right front neck and K30[32:34] sts from back neck st holder. 82[86:90] sts.
Work 22 rows in K1, P1 rib.
Cast (bind) off in rib.
Join left shoulder seam and neckband.
Fold Neckband in half to WS and sew in place.

NELSON COLLAR
Press pieces on WS with a warm iron over a damp cloth, omitting ribbing.
Join shoulder seams.
Work the Neckband and Collar, for the Nelson version only, as foll:
Using set of four double-pointed needles (or short circular needle) and with RS facing, slip first 10[11:12] sts on front st holder onto a spare needle, K rem 10[11:12] sts from st holder, pick up and K15 sts up right front neck, K30[32:34] sts from back

neck st holder and pick up and K15 sts down left front neck, then K10[11:12] sts on st holder. 80[84:88] sts.
Work 8 rounds (RS always facing) in K1, P1 rib, ending at centre front.
To work the Collar, beg at centre front, turn and work in garter st back and forth in rows (K every row) until Collar measures 10cm (4") from beg.
Cast (bind) off all sts.

NAUTILUS NECKBAND
Press pieces on WS with a warm iron over a damp cloth, omitting ribbing.
Join right shoulder seam.
Work the Neckband, for the Nautilus version only, as foll:
Using smaller needles and with RS facing, pick up and K14 sts down left front neck, K20[22:24] sts from st holder, pick up and

K14 sts up right front neck and K30[32:34] sts from back neck st holder. 78[82:86] sts.
Beg with a P row, work 8 rows in st st, so ending with a K (RS) row.
Knit 2 rows to form hemline.
Then beg with a P row, work 6 rows in st st.
Cast (bind) off all sts.
Join left shoulder seam and neckband.
Fold the Neckband in half (along the hemline) to the wrong side and sew loosely in place.

FINISHING
Place markers on Back and Front 22.5[24:25.5]cm (9[9½:10]") from shoulder seam.
Sew Sleeves to Back and Front between markers.
Join side and sleeve seams.
Press seams lightly on WS with a warm iron over a damp cloth, omitting ribbing (and garter st).

These gorgeous sweaters will go well with jeans or they could be dressed up with a winter skirt for those very cold days. They are thick enough for the coldest winter walk.

'So simple and incredibly effective. You'll wear these till you die . . . and maybe beyond.'

The 'vine' pattern across the border is echoed in the travelling vines that are knitted up the sweater in this interesting design.

'Have vine, will travel.'

TRAVELLING VINE

R O W A N S P U N   T W E E D

SIZE
One size only (see page 118) for choosing size)
Finished measurement around bust 144cm (57½") when not stretched (the knitted fabric is very elastic and when slightly stretched will measure about 157cm or 62" around the bust)
See diagram for finished measurements of back, front and sleeves. To lengthen or shorten back and front, or sleeves see page 118.

MATERIALS
Rowan *Rowanspun Tweed*
10 x 100g (3½oz) hanks in Iris (shade no. 757) A
2 x 100g (3½oz) hanks in Ecru (shade no. 765) B
One pair each 4mm (US size 6) and 4½mm (US size 7) needles *or size to obtain correct tension (gauge)*
Set of four 4mm (US size 6) double-pointed needles (or short circular needle of same size)
Cable needle

TENSION (GAUGE)
18 sts and 23 rows to 10cm (4") over st st on 4½mm (US size 7) needles
20 sts and 20 rows to 10cm (4") over colour leaf patt
26-st travelling vine panel measures 12.5cm (5") across when not stretched, and 24-row rep measures 11cm (4¼")
Check your tension (gauge) before beginning.

NOTES
When working leaf motif chart, carry the yarn not in use loosely across back of work, weaving it around working yarn.
Read chart from right to left for

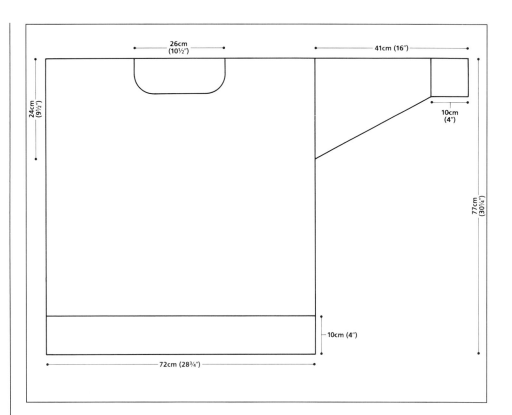

RS (knit) rows and from left to right for WS (purl) rows.

TRAVELLING VINE PANEL
The travelling vine panel is worked over 26 sts to beg, but sts are increased and decreased over the 24-row patt rep so that the number of sts across panel varies.
1st row (WS) K5, P5, K4, P3, K9.
2nd row (RS) P7, P2 tog, *K into front and back of next st – called knit inc –*, K2, P4, K2, *wrap yarn from front to back over top of right-hand needle to form extra loop on right-hand needle – called yo –*, K1, yo, K2, P5.
3rd row K5, P7, K4, P2, K1, P1, K8.
4th row P6, P2 tog, K1, *purl into front and back of next st – called*

purl inc –, K2, P4, K3, yo, K1, yo, K3, P5.
5th row K5, P9, K4, P2, K2, P1, K7.
6th row P5, P2 tog, K1, purl inc, P1, K2, P4, *slip next 2 sts knitwise, one at a time, onto right-hand needle, insert tip of left-hand needle into fronts of 2 slipped sts and K them tog – called ssk –*, K5, K2 tog, P5.
7th row K5, P7, K4, P2, K3, P1, K6.
8th row P4, P2 tog, K1, purl inc, P2, K2, P4, ssk, K3, K2 tog, P5.
9th row K5, P5, K4, P2, K4, P1, K5.
10th row P5, yo, K1, yo, P4, K2, P4, ssk, K1, K2 tog, P5.
11th row K5, P3, K4, P2, K4, P3, K5.
12th row P5, (K1, yo) twice, K1,

P4, K1, *insert left-hand needle from front to back under horizontal strand between st just worked and next st on left-hand needle thus forming loop on left-hand needle and K into back of this loop – called make 1 –*, K1, P2 tog, P2, sl 2 knitwise-K1-p2sso, P5.

13th row K9, P3, K4, P5, K5.
14th row P5, K2, yo, K1, yo, K2, P4, K1, knit inc, K1, P2 tog, P7.
15th row K8, P1, K1, P2, K4, P7, K5.
16th row P5, K3, yo, K1, yo, K3, P4, K2, purl inc, K1, P2 tog, P6.
17th row K7, P1, K2, P2, K4, P9, K5.
18th row P5, ssk, K5, K2 tog, P4, K2, P1, purl inc, K1, P2 tog, P5.
19th row K6, P1, K3, P2, K4, P7, K5.
20th row P5, ssk, K3, K2 tog, P4, K2, P2, purl inc, K1, P2 tog, P4.
21st row K5, P1, K4, P2, K4, P5, K5.
22nd row P5, ssk, K1, K2 tog, P4, K2, P4, yo, K1, yo, P5.
23rd row K5, P3, K4, P2, K4, P3, K5.
24th row P5, sl 2 knitwise-K1-p2sso, P2, P2 tog, K1, make 1, K1, P4, (K1, yo) twice, K1, P5.
These 24 rows are repeated to

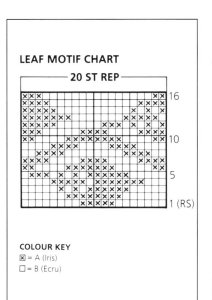

LEAF MOTIF CHART
20 ST REP
16
10
5
1 (RS)

COLOUR KEY
⊠ = A (Iris)
☐ = B (Ecru)

form the travelling vine patt.

BACK
Using smaller needles and yarn A, cast on 140 sts.
Knit one row (WS).
Change to yarn B and beg cable rib as foll:
1st rib row (RS) *P2, K4, rep from * to last 2 sts, P2.
2nd rib row *K2, P4, rep from * to last 2 sts, K2.
3rd rib row *P2, slip next 2 sts onto a cable needle and hold at back of work, K next 2 sts from left-hand needle, then K2 sts from cable needle, rep from * to last 2 sts, P2.
4th rib row As 2nd row.
Rep 3rd and 4th rib rows only until cable rib measures 10cm (4") from beg, ending with a WS row.
Change to larger needles and beg with a K row, work in st st working 2 rows in yarn A, 2 rows in yarn B and 2 rows in yarn A, so ending with a WS row.
Beg with first chart row (K row), work in st st foll leaf motif chart (see *Notes* above), working 20-st rep 7 times across each row, until all 16 rows of chart have been completed, so ending with a WS row.
Beg with a K row and using yarn B, work 2 rows in st st. Break off yarn B.
Using yarn A, work 5 rows in garter st (K every row), so ending with a RS row.
Beg working travelling vine panels on next row as foll:
1st patt row (WS) K14, *P2, work first row of travelling vine patt across next 26 sts, P2, K11, rep from * twice more, but ending last rep K14 instead of K11.
2nd patt row (RS) P14, *K2, work 2nd row of travelling vine patt across next 26 sts, K2, P11, rep from * twice more, but ending last rep P14 instead of P11.
The patt is now set.
Cont in this way until all 24 rows

of travelling vine patt have been completed. Then work 24-row rep 3 times more, so ending with a 24th patt row (RS). 140 sts.
Work first patt row again, so ending with a WS row.***
Beg with a K row and using yarn B, work 2 rows in st st, so ending with a WS row.
Rep from ** to ** once. Break off yarn A.
Beg with a K row and using yarn B, work 2 rows in st st.
Cast (bind) off 44 sts at beg of next 2 rows.
Slip rem 52 sts onto a spare needle for back neck.

FRONT
Work as for Back to ***.
Shape Neck
Beg neck shaping on next row as foll:
Next row (RS) Work 54 sts in patt (2nd patt row), turn leaving rem sts on a spare needle.
Working on first side of neck only, work 3rd-13th patt rows *and at the same time* cast (bind) off 3 sts at beg of next row (neck edge), cast (bind) off 2 sts at neck edge on foll 2 alt rows, then dec one st at neck edge on foll 3 alt rows, so ending with a WS row. 44 sts.
Work 14th-23rd patt rows without shaping, so ending with a WS row. 44 sts.
Cast (bind) off in knit.
Return to rem sts and with RS facing, slip centre 32 sts onto a st holder, rejoin yarn to rem sts and work in patt to end.
Complete 2nd side of neck to match first side, reversing all shaping.

SLEEVES
Using smaller needles and yarn A, cast on 50 sts.
Knit one row (WS).
Change to B and work 10cm (4") in cable rib as for Back, ending with a WS row.
Change to larger needles and beg with a K row, work in st st

working 2 rows in yarn A and 2 rows in yarn B (break off yarn B), then using yarn A work 5 rows in garter st (K every row) *and at the same time* inc one st at each end of next row and every foll alt row. 60 sts.

Beg working travelling vine panel on next row as foll:

1st patt row (WS) K15, P2, work first row of travelling vine patt across next 26 sts, P2, K15.

2nd patt row (RS) P into front and back of first st, P14, K2, work 2nd row of travelling vine patt across next 26 sts, K2, P14, P into front and back of last st.

The patt is now set.

Cont in this way until all 24 rows of travelling vine patt have been completed, work 24-row rep once more and then rep 1st–13th patt rows *and at the same time* cont shaping sleeve by inc one st at each end of every alt row until there are 30 reverse st st sts before K2 rib on right-hand side of RS of Sleeve and 30 reverse st st sts after K2 rib on left-hand side of RS of Sleeve, so ending with a WS row. 90 sts.

Cast (bind) off all sts in knit.

Make 2nd Sleeve in the same way.

NECKBAND

Join shoulder seams, easing in sts across top of travelling vine panel.

Using set of double-pointed needles (or short circular needle) and yarn B and with RS facing, beg at left shoulder seam, pick up and K18 sts down left front neck, K32 sts from st holder, pick up and K18 sts up right front neck and K52 sts from back neck spare needle. 120 sts.

Working in rounds (RS always facing), beg cable rib as foll:

1st rib round (RS) P1, *K4, P2, rep from *, but ending last rep P1 instead of P2.

2nd rib round As first round.

3rd rib round P1, *slip next 2 sts onto a cable needle and hold at

back of work, K next 2 sts from left-hand needle, then K2 sts from cable needle, P2, rep from *, but ending last rep P1 instead of P2.

4th rib round As first round.

Rep 3rd and 4th rib rounds only until cable rib measures 8cm (3") from beg, ending with a 4th rib row.

Using B, cast (bind) off loosely in K4, P2 rib.

FINISHING

Place markers on Back and Front 24cm (9½") from shoulder seam. Sew Sleeves to Back and Front between markers, easing in sts across top of travelling vine panel.

Join side and sleeve seams. Press seams lightly on WS with a warm iron over a damp cloth, *but omitting cable ribbing and travelling vine panels.*

MOSS STITCH BLAZER

ROWAN MAGPIE ARAN

SIZES
To choose appropriate size see page 118
Finished measurement around bust 134[160]cm (53½[64]")
Figures for larger size are given in brackets; where there is only one set of figures, it applies to both sizes.
See diagram for finished measurements of back, fronts and sleeves. To lengthen or shorten back and fronts, or sleeves see page 118.

MATERIALS
12[13] x 100g (3½oz) hanks of Rowan *Magpie Aran* in Sea Lord (shade no. 608) *or* Admiral (shade no. 504) A
6 x 25g (1oz) hanks of Rowan *Lightweight DK* in Rust (shade no. 27) B
One pair each 4½mm (US size 7) and 5½mm (US size 9) needles *or size to obtain correct tension (gauge)*

TENSION (GAUGE)
15 sts and 22 rows to 10cm (4") over double moss st patt on 5½mm (US size 9) needles and using yarn A
16 sts and 26 rows to 10cm (4") over double moss st patt on 4½mm (US size 7) needles and using yarn A
Check your tension (gauge) before beginning.

NOTES
The blazer can be worked in either Sealord or Admiral, but the piping colour remains the same. When working piping, use yarn B double.

DOUBLE MOSS STITCH
Worked over a multiple of 4 sts.
1st row *K2, P2, rep from * to end.
2nd row As first row.
3rd row *P2, K2, rep from * to end.
4th row As 3rd row.
These 4 rows are rep to form double moss stitch patt.

BACK
Using smaller needles and yarn A, cast on 100[120] sts.
Work 10cm (4") in double moss stitch patt.
Change to larger needles and cont in double moss st until Back measures 50.5[54]cm (20[21½]") from beg.
Shape Armholes
Cont in double moss st through-out and keeping patt correct,

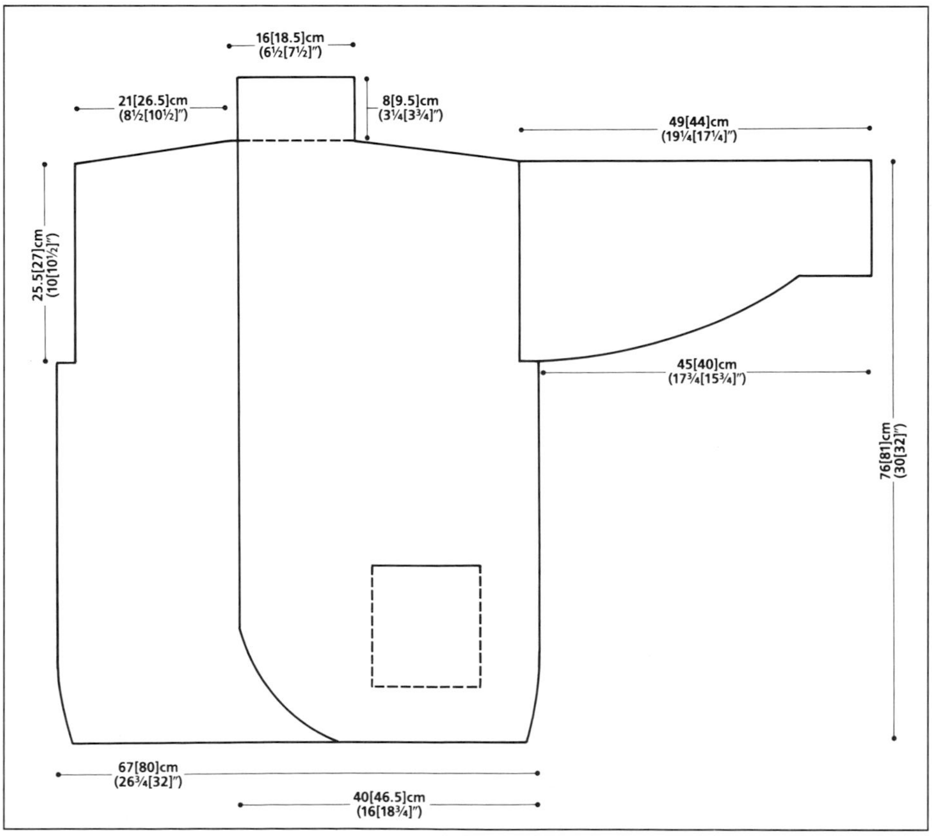

16[18.5]cm (6½[7½]")

21[26.5]cm (8½[10½]")

8[9.5]cm (3¼[3¾]")

49[44]cm (19¼[17¼]")

25.5[27]cm (10[10½]")

45[40]cm (17¾[15¾]")

76[81]cm (30[32]")

67[80]cm (26¾[32]")

40[46.5]cm (16[18¾]")

Make one of these and you'll never want to part with it, knitted in Aran-weight wool with contrast trim.

'Not a blazer at all, but a fantastic versatile throw-on.'

'Not a blazer at all, but a fantastic versatile throw-on.'

cast (bind) off 6 sts at beg of next 2 rows. 88[108] sts.
Work without shaping until Back measures 76[81]cm (30[32]") from beg.

Shape Shoulders
Cast (bind) off 12[14] sts at beg of next 2 rows, then cast (bind) off 10[13] sts at beg of next 4 rows.
Cast (bind) off rem 24[28] sts for back neck.

LEFT FRONT
Before beg Left Front, make pocket lining.

Pocket Lining
Using larger needles and yarn A, cast on 24 sts.
Work 17cm (7") in double moss st patt.
Do not break off yarn and slip sts onto a st holder, setting aside to be used later.
Beg Left Front as foll:
Using smaller needles and yarn A, cast on 44[52] sts.

Work first row of double moss st patt.
Cont in double moss st throughout and keeping patt correct, inc one st at beg (centre front edge) of next row and at centre front edge on every foll alt row until Left Front measures 10cm (4") from beg.
Change to larger needles and cont inc one st at centre front edge on every alt row until there are 60[70] sts.
Work without shaping until Left Front measures 24[26.5]cm (9½ [10½]") from beg, ending at centre front edge (shaped edge).

Place Pocket
Place pocket as foll:
Next row Work 24[30] sts in patt, cast (bind) off next 24 sts, work in patt to end.
Next row Work first 12[16] sts in patt, then work in patt across 24 sts of pocket lining (adjusting pocket-lining rows if necessary before working sts so that patt matches), work in patt across rem sts of Left Front.
Cont without shaping until Left Front measures same as Back to armhole, ending at side seam edge (straight edge).

Shape Armhole
Cast (bind) off 6 sts at beg of next row. 54[64] sts.
Work without shaping until Left Front measures same as Back to shoulder, ending at armhole edge.

Shape Shoulder
Cast (bind) off 12[14] sts at beg of next row, work one row without shaping, then cast (bind) off 10[13] sts at beg of next and foll alt row.
Work without shaping on rem 22[24] sts for Collar for 8[9.5]cm (3¼[3¾]") more.
Cast (bind) off.

RIGHT FRONT
The double moss stitch pattern is reversible, so work the Right Front in exactly the same way as the Left Front was worked.

SLEEVES
Using smaller needles and yarn A, cast on 48 sts.
Work 10cm (4") in double moss st patt.
Change to larger needles and then cont in double moss st throughout, inc one st at each end of next and every foll 4th[3rd] row until there are 76[80] sts, keeping patt correct throughout.
Work without shaping until Sleeve measures 49[44]cm (19¼ [17¼]") from beg.
Cast (bind) off all sts.
Make 2nd Sleeve in the same way.

FINISHING
Do not press.
Join shoulder seams. Sew cast- (bound-) off edge of Sleeves to vertical edge of armholes and sew cast- (bound-) off edge of armhole shaping to sides of Sleeves.
Join side and sleeve seams.
Join cast- (bound-) off edges of Collar. Then sew Collar to back neck.

Piping
Using smaller needles and yarn B double throughout, cast on 8 sts.
Work in st st until piping, when slightly stretched, is long enough to fit from centre back cast-on edge, around to Right Front, up centre front, along Collar, then down Left Front and around to centre back to meet cast-on edge of piping. Slip sts onto st holder, but do not break off yarn. Pin piping in place along edge, overlapping edge of garment slightly on RS and WS and allowing knitted fabric to roll. Adjust length of piping as necessary and cast (bind) off. Join ends of piping tog and sew piping in place.
Work a length of piping in the same way for each sleeve end and for each pocket top and sew in place. Sew pocket linings to WS of Fronts.

BLUE DAYS JACKET

R O W A N   C H U N K Y   T W E E D

SIZE
One size only (see page 118 for choosing size)
Finished measurement around bust 159cm (63½")
See diagram for finished measurements of back, fronts and sleeves. To lengthen or shorten back and fronts, or sleeves see page 118.

MATERIALS
18 x 100g (3½oz) hanks of Rowan *Chunky Tweed* in Blue Days (shade no. 703)
One pair each 4½mm (US size 7) and 5½mm (US size 9) needles *or size to obtain correct tension (gauge)*
Seven 2.5cm (1") buttons
Two stitch markers

TENSION (GAUGE)
15½ sts and 24 rows to 10cm (4") over diagonal patt on 5½mm (US size 9) needles
15 sts and 26 rows (unstretched) to 10cm (4") over ridge patt (for sleeves) on 5½mm (US size 9) needles
Check your tension (gauge) before beginning.

BACK
Using smaller needles, cast on 124 sts.
Beg K2, P2 rib as foll:
1st rib row *K2, P2, rep from * to end.
Rep last row until ribbing measures 10cm (4") from beg, dec one st at end of last row. 123 sts.
Change to larger needles and work 4 rows in garter st (knit every row).
Beg diagonal patt as foll:
1st patt row (RS) P1, K2, (P2, K2) 14 times, P1; slip st marker onto right-hand needle, P1, K1 (centre st), P1, slip st marker onto right-hand needle; P1, K2, (P2, K2) 14 times, P1.
2nd row (K2, P2) 15 times; slip marker, K1, P1, K1, slip marker; (P2, K2) 15 times.
3rd row K1, P2, (K2, P2) 14 times, K1; slip marker, P1, K1, P1, slip marker; K1, P2, (K2, P2) 14 times, K1.
4th row (P2, K2) 15 times; slip marker, K1, P1, K1, slip marker; (K2, P2) 15 times.
Rep first-4th rows of diagonal patt as just set until Back

measures 48.5cm (19") from beg, ending with a WS row.
Knit 2 rows to beg garter-st ridge.
Shape Armholes
Cont in garter st (knit every row), cast (bind) off 10 sts at beg of next 2 rows. 103 sts.
Knit one row, so ending with a RS row.
Beg the diamond pattern on the next row as foll:
1st patt row (WS) P2, K3, *P9, K3, rep from *, ending with P2.
2nd row K4, *P2, K7, P2, K1, rep from *, ending last rep K4

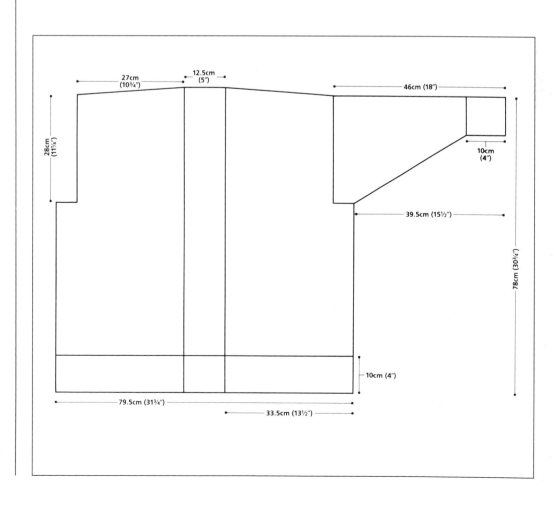

A complicated-looking de-
sign that is in fact very
simple to knit with chunky
wool in a lovely soft colour.

*This one is perfect for long
walks in the woods, or just a
fondle on the doorstep if you
prefer (and I do).*

instead of K1.

3rd row P5, *K2, P5, K2, P3, rep from *, ending last rep P5 instead of P3.

4th row K6, *P2, K3, P2, K5, rep from *, ending last rep K6 instead of K5.

5th row P7, *K2, P1, K2, P7, rep from * to end.

6th row K8, *P3, K9, rep from *, ending last rep K8 instead of K9.

7th row P8, *K3, P9, rep from *, ending last rep P8 instead of P9.

8th row K7, *P2, K1, P2, K7, rep from * to end.

9th row P6, *K2, P3, K2, P5, rep from *, ending last rep P6 instead of P5.

10th row K5, *P2, K5, P2, K3, rep from *, ending last rep K5 instead of K3.

11th row P4, *K2, P7, K2, P1, rep from *, ending last rep P4 instead of P1.

12th row K2, P3, *K9, P3, rep from *, ending with K2.

Rep first-12th rows of diamond patt as just set until Back measures 78cm (31") from beg, ending with a WS row.

Shape Shoulders

Keeping to diamond patt as set, cast (bind) off 14 sts at beg of next 6 rows.

Cast (bind) off rem 19 sts for back neck.

LEFT FRONT

**Using smaller needles, cast on 52 sts.

Work 10cm (4") in K2, P2 rib as for Back.

Change to larger needles and work 4 rows in garter st (knit every row).**

Beg diagonal patt as foll:

1st patt row (RS) P1, K2, *P2, K2, rep from *, ending with P1.

2nd row *P2, K2, rep from * to end.

3rd row K1, P2, *K2, P2, rep from *, ending with K1.

4th row *K2, P2, rep from * to end.

Rep first-4th rows of diagonal

patt as just set until Right Front measures 20cm (8") from beg, ending with a WS row.

Pocket Opening

Divide for pocket opening on next row as foll:

Next row (RS) Work 13 sts in diagonal patt, inc in next st, turn leaving rem 38 sts on a st holder. Working first set of sts only and keeping diagonal patt correct as set, inc one st at beg of next row (pocket edge) and then inc one st at pocket edge on every foll row until there are 36 sts, so ending with a WS row.

Do not break off yarn, but slip these sts onto a st holder and set aside.

Return to rem 38 sts and with RS facing, rejoin yarn and keeping diagonal patt correct as set, dec one st at beg of next row (pocket edge) and then dec one st at pocket edge on every foll row until 16 sts rem, so ending with a WS row.

Break off yarn and slip these 16 sts onto a spare needle.

Join sides of pocket opening on next row as foll:

Return to 36 sts on st holder and with RS facing, work in patt as set across these 36 sts, then cont in patt across 16 sts on spare needle. 52 sts.

Cont in diagonal patt without shaping until Left Front measures same as Back to garter-st ridge at armhole, ending with a WS row. Knit 2 rows, so ending with a WS row.

Shape Armhole

Cont in garter st (knit every row), cast (bind) off 10 sts at beg of next row. 42 sts.

Knit 2 rows more, so ending with a RS row.

Beg diamond patt as foll:

1st patt row (WS) P1, K3, *P9, K3, rep from *, ending with P2.

2nd row K4, *P2, K7, P2, K1, rep from *, ending last rep K3 instead of K1.

3rd row P4, *K2, P5, K2, P3, rep from *, ending last rep P5

instead of P3.

4th row K6, *P2, K3, P2, K5, rep from * to end.

5th row P6, *K2, P1, K2, P7, rep from * to end.

6th row K8, *P3, K9, rep from *, ending last rep K7 instead of K9.

7th row P7, *K3, P9, rep from *, ending last rep P8 instead of P9.

8th row K7, *P2, K1, P2, K7, rep from *, ending last rep K6 instead of K7.

9th row P5, *K2, P3, K2, P5, rep from *, ending last rep P6 instead of P5.

10th row K5, *P2, K5, P2, K3, rep from *, ending last rep K4 instead of K3.

11th row P3, *K2, P7, K2, P1, rep from *, ending last rep P4 instead of P1.

12th row K2, P3, *K9, P3, rep from *, ending with K1.

Rep first-12th rows of diamond patt as just set until Left Front measures same as Back to shoulder, ending with a WS row (at armhole edge).

Shape Shoulder

Keeping to diamond patt as set, cast (bind) off 14 sts at beg of next and foll alt row, work one row without shaping, then cast (bind) off rem 14 sts.

RIGHT FRONT

Work as for Left Front from ** to **.

Beg diagonal patt as foll:

1st patt row (RS) P1, K2, *P2, K2, rep from *, ending with P1.

2nd row *K2, P2, rep from * to end.

3rd row K1, P2, *K2, P2, rep from *, ending with K1.

4th row *P2, K2, rep from * to end.

Rep first-4th rows of diagonal patt as just set until Right Front measures 20cm (8") from beg, ending with a WS row.

Pocket Opening

Divide for pocket opening on next row as foll:

Next row (RS) Work 36 sts in

diagonal patt, K2 tog, turn leaving rem 14 sts on a st holder. Working first set of sts only and keeping diagonal patt correct as set, dec one st at beg of next row (pocket edge) and then dec one st at pocket edge on every foll row until 16 sts rem, so ending with a WS row.

Do not break off yarn, but slip these 16 sts onto a st holder and set aside.

Return to rem 14 sts and with RS facing, rejoin yarn and keeping diagonal patt correct as set, inc one st at beg of next row (pocket edge) and then inc one st at pocket edge on every foll row until there are 36 sts, so ending with a WS row.

Break off yarn and slip these 36 sts onto a spare needle.

Join sides of pocket opening on next row as foll:

Return to 16 sts on st holder and with RS facing, work in patt as set across these 16 sts, then cont in patt across 36 sts on spare needle. 52 sts.

Cont in diagonal patt without shaping until Right Front measures same as Back to garter-st ridge at armhole, ending with a WS row.

Knit 3 rows, so ending with a RS row.

Shape Armhole

Cont in garter st (knit every row), cast (bind) off 10 sts at beg of next row. 42 sts.

Knit one row more, so ending with a RS row.

Beg diamond patt as foll:

1st patt row (WS) P2, K3, *P9, K3, rep from *, ending with P1.

2nd row K3, *P2, K7, P2, K1, rep from *, ending last rep K4 instead of K1.

3rd row P5, *K2, P5, K2, P3, rep from *, ending last rep P4 instead of P3.

4th row K5, *P2, K3, P2, K5, rep from *, ending last rep K6 instead of K5.

5th row P7, *K2, P1, K2, P7, rep from *, ending last rep P6

instead of P7.

6th row K7, *P3, K9, rep from *, ending last rep K8 instead of K9.

7th row P8, *K3, P9, rep from *, ending last rep P7 instead of P9.

8th row K6, *P2, K1, P2, K7, rep from * to end.

9th row P6, *K2, P3, K2, P5, rep from * to end.

10th row K4, *P2, K5, P2, K3, rep from *, ending last rep K5 instead of K3.

11th row P4, *K2, P7, K2, P1, rep from *, ending last rep P3 instead of P1.

12th row K1, P3, *K9, P3, rep from *, ending with K2.

Rep first-12th rows of diamond patt as just set until Right Front measures same as Back to shoulder, ending with a RS row (at armhole edge).

Shape shoulder as for Left Front.

SLEEVES

Using smaller needles, cast on 44 sts.

Work 10cm (4") in K2, P2 rib as for Back.

Change to larger needles and beg ridge patt as foll:

Knit one row (RS), inc one st at each end of row. 46 sts.

Purl 2 rows, then knit 2 rows, inc one st at each end of last row. 48 sts.

Cont in ridge patt by rep from * to * *and at the same time* shape Sleeve by inc one st at each end of 3rd and 4th rows alt until there are 84 sts.

Cont in ridge patt as set without shaping until Sleeve measures 46cm (18") from beg.

Cast (bind) off all sts.

Make 2nd Sleeve in the same way.

POCKET LININGS

Beg left-front pocket lining as foll:

Using larger needles, cast on 22 sts.

Work in st st until lining measures 10cm (4") from beg,

ending with a P row (WS).

Cont in st st throughout, dec one st at beg of next row and then dec one st at same edge on every row until 2 sts rem.

Cast (bind) off.

With RS of lining facing WS of Left Front, sew shaped edge of lining to top edge of pocket opening, then sew rem 3 sides to WS of Front.

Make right-front pocket lining in the same way, but reversing shaping, and sew to Right Front.

LEFT-FRONT BAND

Join shoulder seams.

Beg left-front Band (which forms button band and one half of collar) as foll:

Using smaller needles, cast on 30 sts.

Knit one row (WS).

Purl 2 rows, then knit 2 rows, so ending with a WS row.

Work single buttonhole of left-front Band on next row as foll:

1st buttonhole row (RS) P24, cast (bind) off 2 sts, P to end.

2nd buttonhole row P4, cast on 2 sts, P to end.

Knit 2 rows.

Cont in ridge patt by rep from * to * until Band, when slightly stretched, fits up Left Front to shoulder seam and, when unstretched, across to centre back neck.

Do not cast (bind) off and do not break off yarn.

Remembering to position Band so that buttonhole is on outside edge at beg of Band, sew Band in place along centre edge of Left Front and across to centre back neck, adjusting length as necessary before casting (binding) off.

Mark positions for 6 buttons on Band; the first at same level as buttonhole already worked but 4.5cm (1¾") from seam joining Band to Left Front, the top 22cm (8¾") from cast-on edge of Band and the rem 4 buttons evenly spaced between.

RIGHT-FRONT BAND
Beg right-front Band (which forms buttonhole band and 2nd half of collar) as foll:
Using smaller needles, cast on 30 sts.
Knit one row (WS).
Purl 2 rows, then knit 2 rows, so ending with a WS row.
Work first buttonhole of right-front Band on next row as foll:
1st buttonhole row (RS) P6, cast (bind) off 2 sts, P to end.
2nd buttonhole row P22, cast on 2 sts, P to end.
Complete as for left-front Band, making butthonholes as for first buttonhole on right-front Band to correspond with markers.
With buttonholes on outside edge at beg of Band, sew Band in place along centre edge of Right Front and across to centre back neck, adjusting length as necessary before casting (binding) off.

FINISHING
Do not press pieces.
Join cast- (bound-) off edges of Collar.
Pocket Tops
Using smaller needles and with RS facing, pick up and K28 sts evenly across edge of left-front pocket opening. Work 3cm (1¼") in K1, P1 rib.
Cast (bind) off in rib.
Work top across right-front pocket opening in the same way.
Sew ends of pocket tops to RS of Fronts.
Sew cast- (bound-) off edge of Sleeves to vertical edge of armholes and sew cast- (bound-) off edge of armhole shaping to sides of Sleeves.
Sew 6 buttons to left-front Band to correspond to 6 buttonholes on right-front Band. Sew 7th button to WS of right-front Band to correspond to single buttonhole on left-front Band.
Press seams *only* lightly on WS side with a warm iron over a damp cloth.

EVENING WEAR

Silk, style, glamour and pearls — what else do you need to create a sensation? Whether it's an evening out or entertaining at home, you'll look and feel wonderful.

Knitted in soft mohair this sweater can be worn in a variety of ways, either closer to the neck or dare to be bare!

'Don't forget to take your bra strap off for the full, Breakfast at Tiffany's effect!'

SOFT FOCUS

ROWAN KID/SILK

SIZES

To choose appropriate size see page 118
Finished measurement around bust 124[150]cm (49½[60]")
Figures for larger size are given in brackets; where there is only one set of figures, it applies to both sizes.
See diagram for finished measurements of back, front and sleeves. To lengthen or shorten back and front, or sleeves see page 118.

MATERIALS

Rowan *Kid/Silk*
9[11] x 50g (1¾oz) balls in Garnet (shade no. 992) A
1 x 50g (1¾oz) ball in Natural (shade no. 977) B
One pair each 4mm (US size 6) and 4½mm (US size 7) needles *or size to obtain correct tension (gauge)*
5.50mm (size I) crochet hook

TENSION (GAUGE)

19 sts and 24 rows to 10cm (4") over st st on 4½mm (US size 7) needles
Check your tension (gauge) before beginning.

BACK

Using smaller needles and yarn A, cast on 118[142] sts.
Work 10cm (4") in K1, P1 rib.
Change to larger needles and beg with a K row, work in st st until Back measures 52[57]cm (20½[22½]") from beg, ending with a WS row.

Shape Neck
Beg neck shaping on next row as foll:
Next row (RS) K37[43], turn leaving all of the rem sts on a spare needle.

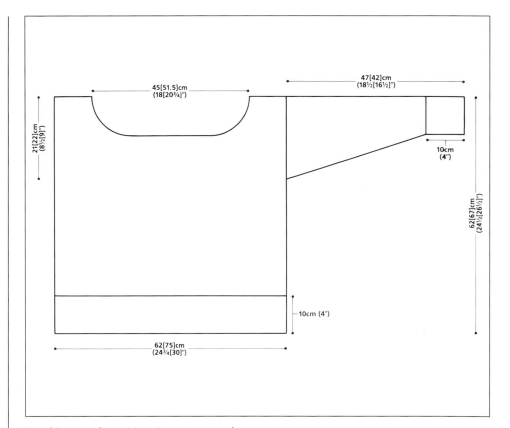

Working on first side of neck only and **cont in st st throughout, cast (bind) off 3 sts at beg of next row (neck edge), then cast (bind) off at neck edge 3 sts on 2 foll alt rows and 2 sts on 3 foll alt rows. 22[28] sts.
Work one row without shaping.
Dec one st at neck edge on next and every foll alt row 6 times in all. 16[22] sts.**
Work one row without shaping, so ending with a RS row.
Cast (bind) off.
Return to rem sts and with RS facing, rejoin yarn A and cast (bind) off centre 44[56] sts, then K to end of row.
Work one row without shaping.
Rep from ** to ** as for first side to complete 2nd side of neck, so

ending with a RS row.
Cast (bind) off rem sts.

FRONT
Work as for Back.

SLEEVES
Using smaller needles and yarn A,
cast on 48[52] sts.
Work 10cm (4") in K1, P1 rib.
Change to larger needles and
beg with a K row, work 2 rows in
st st.
Cont in st st throughout, inc one
st at each end of next and every
foll 4th[3rd] row until there are
80[84] sts.
Work without shaping until
Sleeve measures 47[42]cm
(18½[16½]") from beg, ending
with a WS row.
Cast (bind) off all sts.
Make 2nd Sleeve in the same
way.

COLLAR
Do not join shoulder seams, but
beg working one half of Collar
across Back as foll:
Using smaller needles and yarn A
and with RS facing, pick up and
K22 sts down left back neck,
44[56] sts across centre back
neck and K22 sts up right back
neck. 88[100] sts.
Work 3 rows in K1, P1 rib, so
ending with a WS row.
Cont in K1, P1 rib throughout,
dec one st at each end of next
and every foll 4th row 8 times in
all. 72[84] sts.
Work without shaping (if
necessary) until Collar measures
13cm (5") from beg.
Cast (bind) off in rib.
Work 2nd half of Collar across
Front in the same way.

FINISHING
Using crochet hook and yarn B,
make a chain 220cm (86½")
long. Do not break off yarn.
Pin chain in place along back
neck edge (below ribbing) from
shoulder seam edge to shoulder
seam edge, forming 7 oval loops

6cm (2¼") wide by 7.5cm (3")
long and placing first oval 4cm
(1½") from right shoulder and 7th
oval 4cm (1½") from left shoulder
and 5 rem ovals 4cm (1½") apart
(see photograph of garment).
Adjust length of chain as
necessary, then fasten off. Using
yarn B, sew chain in place
through holes in chain.
Work a 2nd chain and sew it
along the front neck edge in the
same way.

Press pieces lightly on WS with a
warm iron over a damp cloth,
omitting ribbing.
Join shoulder seams and Collar,
matching chain at shoulders.
Place markers on Back and Front
21[22]cm (8½[9]") from shoulder
seam.
Sew Sleeves to Back and Front
between markers.
Join side and sleeve seams.
Press seams lightly on WS with a
warm iron over a damp cloth.

EVENING PEARLS

R O W A N   S I L K   A N D   W O O L

SIZE
One size only (see page 118 for choosing size)
Finished measurement around bust 144cm (58")
See diagram for finished measurements of back, front and sleeves. To lengthen or shorten back and front see page 118.

MATERIALS
42 x 25g (1oz) balls of Rowan *Silk and Wool* in Camel (shade no. 851)
One pair each 3¾mm (US size 5) and 4½mm (US size 7) needles *or size to obtain correct tension (gauge)*
Set of four 3¾mm (US size 5) double-pointed needles (or short circular needle of same size)
Two stitch markers
556 pearl beads 5mm in diameter

TENSION (GAUGE)
21 sts and 27 rows to 10cm (4") over st st on 4½mm (US size 7) needles and using yarn double throughout
Check your tension (gauge) before beginning.

NOTES
*Use yarn double throughout.
Begin the garment by working the back and front. Then work the sleeves and yoke in one piece, working the lozenge pattern panel across the piece as instructed.
Beads are sewn on after pieces have been knitted. (See page 125 for where to purchase beads.)*

KNIT AND PURL TWISTS
(Refer to the following instructions when working the lozenge pattern panel.)

Twist-stitches form outlines around lozenge patt are worked as foll:
K2T *(knit 2 twist)* – skip the next st on left-hand needle and, working in front of skipped st, K the 2nd st on left-hand needle, then K the skipped st and slip both sts from the left-hand needle tog.
K2TB *(knit 2 twist back)* – skip the next st on left-hand needle and, working behind skipped st, K through back of loop of the 2nd st on left-hand needle, then K the skipped st in the usual way and slip both sts from the left-hand needle tog.
P2T *(purl 2 twist)* – skip the next st on left-hand needle and, working in front of skipped st, P the 2nd st on left-hand needle,

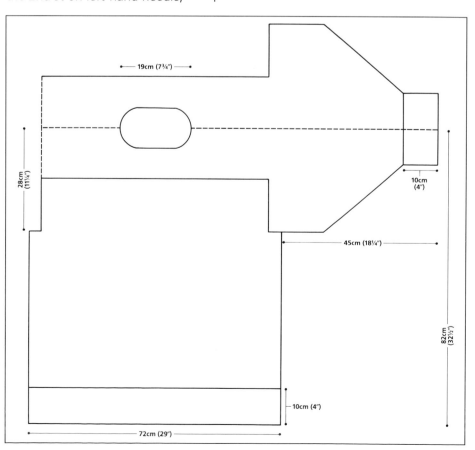

then P the skipped st and slip both sts from the left-hand needle tog.

P2TB *(purl 2 twist back)* – skip the next st on left-hand needle and, working behind skipped st, P through back of loop of the 2nd st on left-hand needle, then P the skipped st in the usual way and slip both sts from the left-hand needle tog.

LOZENGE PATTERN PANEL

(Refer to these instructions when working the yoke and sleeves.) The lozenge patt is worked over panel of 50 sts as foll:

1st row (RS) K2TB *(see instructions for twist sts above)*, (K1, P1) 23 times, K2T.
2nd row P1, P2T, (K1, P1) 22 times, P2TB, P1.
3rd row K2, K2TB, (K1, P1) 21 times, K2T, K2.
4th row P3, P2T, (K1, P1) 20 times, P2TB, P3.
5th row K4, K2TB, (K1, P1) 19 times, K2T, K4.
6th row P5, P2T, (K1, P1) 18 times, P2TB, P5.
Cont in this way, working one st more in st st on each side of lozenge shape on each row and working twist sts on RS and WS as set with 2 sts less of moss (seed) st between twist-st outlines on each row, until there are only 4 sts of moss (seed) st between twist sts (22nd row has been worked). Then cont as foll:
23rd row K22, K2TB, K1, P1, K2T, K22.
24th row P23, P2T, P2TB, P23.
25th row K24, K2T, K24.
26th row P22, P2TB, P1, K1, P2T, P22.
27th row K21, K2T, (P1, K1) twice, K2TB, K21.
28th row P20, P2TB, (P1, K1) 3 times, P2T, P20.
29th row K19, K2T, (P1, K1) 4 times, K2TB, K19.
30th row P18, P2TB, (P1, K1) 5 times, P2T, P18.
Cont in this way, working one st less in st st on each side of

lozenge shape on each row, working twist sts on RS and WS as set with 2 sts more of moss (seed) st between twist-st outlines on each row, until there are 42 sts of moss (seed) st between twist sts (46th row has been worked). Then cont as foll:
47th row K1, K2T, (P1, K1) 22 times, K2TB, K1.
48th row P2TB, (P1, K1) 23 times, P2T.
These 48 rows are rep to form lozenge patt.

BACK

Using smaller needles and using yarn double, cast on 150 sts.
Beg broken diagonal rib as foll:
1st rib row (RS) *K4, P2, rep from * to end.
2nd rib row *K2, P4, rep from * to end.
3rd and 4th rib rows As first and 2nd rows.
5th rib row K2, *P2, K4, rep from * to last 4 sts, P2, K2.
6th rib row P2, *K2, P4, rep from * to last 4 sts, K2, P2.
7th and 8th rib rows As 5th and 6th rows.
9th rib row *P2, K4, rep from * to end.
10th rib row *P4, K2, rep from * to end.
11th and 12th rib rows As 9th and 10th rows.
Rep last 12 rows until rib measures 10cm (4") from beg, ending with a WS and inc one st at each end of last row. 152 sts.
Change to larger needles and beg with a K row, work in st st until Back measures 54cm (21¼") from beg, ending with a WS row.
Shape Armholes
Cont in st st throughout, cast (bind) off 8 sts at beg of next 2 rows. 136 sts.
Work without shaping until Back measures 68cm (27") from beg, ending with a WS row.
Cast (bind) off all sts.

FRONT

Work the Front as for Back.

SLEEVES AND YOKE

Sleeves and Yoke are worked in one piece from cuff to cuff.
Using smaller needles and using yarn double, cast on 48 sts.
Work 10cm (4") in broken diagonal rib as for Back, ending with a RS row.
Working in diagonal rib as set, inc 10 sts across last rib row as foll:
Next row (inc row) (WS) *Rib 4, *work into front and back of next st – called inc 1 –*, rep from * 8 times more, rib 2, inc 1 in last st. 58 sts.
Change to larger needles, and beg lozenge patt across panel of 50 sts, working st st on each side of panel as foll:
1st row (RS) K4; slip st marker onto right-hand needle, work next 50 sts as for first row of lozenge patt panel, slip st marker onto right-hand needle; K4.
2nd row P4; slip marker, work next 50 sts as for 2nd row of lozenge patt panel, slip marker; P4.
This sets position of lozenge patt.
Cont foll lozenge patt across 50 sts between markers *and at the same time* shape Sleeve by inc one st at each end of next and every foll alt row until there are 122 sts, then cont without shaping *and at the same time* cont foll lozenge patt across 50 sts between markers until 48th patt row has been completed, work first-48th rows once more, then work first-10th patt row, so ending with a WS row.
Keeping to patt as set, cast (bind) off 32 sts beg of next 2 rows (11th and 12th patt rows). 58 sts.
Cont on these 58 sts, working 13th-48th patt rows, then first-16th patt rows, so ending with a WS row.
Shape Neck
Beg shaping neck on next row (17th patt row) as foll:
Next row (RS) Work 27 sts in patt, turn leaving rem sts on a spare needle.

Pearls and silk, sheer luxury.

'I thought pearls on knitwear was a huge no-no but this looks fantastic on Jane. (The photographer asked her out for a date after this picture, incidentally.)'

Working on first side of neck only and beg with a P row, cont in st st only and (bind) off 2 sts at beg of next row, then dec one st at neck edge on every row 9 times, so ending with a RS row. 16 sts. Work 4 rows in st st without shaping, so ending with a RS row.
Beg small triangle on next row as foll:
Next row (WS) P2T, P14.
Next row K13, K2T, P1.
Next row P1, K1, P2T, P12.
Next row K11, K2T, P1, K1, P1.
Next row (P1, K1) twice, P2T, P10.
Next row K9, K2T, (P1, K1) twice, P1.
Next row (P1, K1) 3 times, P2T, P8.
Cont in this way, working one st less in st st outside triangle shape on each row and working twist sts on RS and WS as set with one st more of moss (seed) st on each row, until 4 rows more have been worked and there are 10 sts of moss (seed) st on one side of twist sts and 4 sts of st st on the other side, so ending with a WS row. Then cont as foll:
Next row (RS) K4, K2TB, (K1, P1) 5 times.
Next row P1, (K1, P1) 4 times, P2TB, P5.
Cont in this way, working one st more in st st outside triangle shape on each row and working twist sts on RS and WS as set with one st less of moss (seed) st on each row, until 9 rows more have been worked and there are no more moss (seed) sts on one side of twist sts and 14 sts of st st on other side, so ending with a RS row.
This completes small triangle.
Beg with a P row, work 3 rows in st st, so ending with a WS row.
Cont in st st, inc one st at neck edge every row 9 times, then cast on 2 sts at beg of next row, so ending with a WS row. 27 sts.
Do not break off yarn but set these sts aside.

Return to rem sts and with RS facing, cast (bind) off centre 4 sts in moss (seed) st and work in moss (seed) st over next 5 sts including st already on right-hand needle after cast (bind) off, K2T, then K to end.
Purl one row.
Beg with a K row, cont in st st and cast (bind) off 2 sts at beg of next row, then dec one st at neck edge on every row 9 times, so ending with a WS row. 16 sts. Work 3 rows in st st without shaping, so ending with a RS row.
Beg small triangle on next row as foll:
Next row (WS) P14, P2TB.
Next row K1, K2TB, K13.
Next row P12, P2TB, P1, K1.
Next row K1, P1, K1, K2TB, K11.
Next row P10, P2TB, (P1, K1) twice.
Next row (K1, P1) twice, K1, K2TB, K9.
Next row P8, P2TB, (P1, K1) 3 times.
Cont in this way, working one st less in st st outside triangle shape on each row and working twist sts on RS and WS as set with one st more of moss (seed) st on each row, until 4 rows more have been worked and there are 10 sts of moss (seed) st on one side of twist sts and 4 sts of st st on the other side, so ending with a WS row. Then cont as foll:
Next row (RS) (K1, P1) 5 times, K2T, K4.
Next row P5, P2T, K1, (P1, K1) 4 times.
Cont in this way, working one st more in st st outside triangle shape on each row and working twist sts on RS and WS as set with one st less of moss (seed) st on each row, until 9 rows more have been worked and there are no more moss (seed) sts on one side of twist sts and 14 sts of st st on other side, so ending with a RS row.
This completes small triangle.
Beg with a P row, work 2 rows in

st st, so ending with a RS row.
Cont in st st, inc one st at neck edge every row 9 times, then cast on 2 sts at beg of next row, so ending with a RS row. 27 sts. Purl one row. Break off yarn.
Join both sides of Yoke on next row as foll:
Next row With RS facing, K27 sts on first side of neck, cast on 4 sts, K27 sts on other side of neck. 58 sts.
Beg lozenge patt as foll (32nd patt row):
Next row P4; then for 50-st panel work P16, P2TB, (P1, K1) 7 times, P2T, P16 to complete panel; P4.
Next row K4; then for 50-st panel work K15, K2T, (P1, K1) 8 times, K2TB, K15 to complete panel; K4.
Cont in lozenge patt as set. Work 51 rows.
Shape 2nd Sleeve by casting on 32 sts at beg of next 2 rows. 122 sts. Work 42 rows. Dec one st at each end of next and every foll alt row until 58 sts rem, ending with a 48th patt row (WS).
Removing st markers on next row, beg broken diagonal rib as foll:
Next row (RS) K2 tog, K3, P2 tog, P1, (K2 tog, K3, P2) 6 times, K2 tog, K3, P2 tog, P1. 48 sts.
Beg with 2nd rib row as for Back, cont in broken diagonal rib until cuff measures 10cm (4") from beg.
Cast (bind) off in rib patt.

NECKBAND
Using set of double-pointed needles (or short circular needle) and with RS facing, beg at shoulder line and pick up and K16 sts down shaped edge of neck, 22 sts across straight edge of centre neck, 16 sts up shaped edge of neck to shoulder line, 16 sts down shaped section of neck, 22 sts across straight edge of centre neck and 16 sts up shaped edge of neck to beg. 108 sts.
Working in rounds (RS always

facing), beg ribbing on the next round as foll:
Next round (RS) P1, (K4, P2) 17 times, K4, P1.
Rep last round 8 times more to complete the Neckband.
Cast (bind) off *loosely* in rib.

FINISHING

Press pieces lightly on WS, following instructions on yarn label and omitting moss (seed) st and broken diagonal ribbing when pressing.

Apply Beads

Allowing approximately 75 beads for each of the 6 lozenges, 38 beads for each of the 2 half lozenges at cuffs and 15 beads for each of the 2 triangles at the neck, sew on the beads carefully as foll:

Using a needle fine enough to pass easily through the bead and a single strand of yarn, sew the beads to the lozenges in vertical rows up and down the lozenges in the direction of the knitting (in this way the lines of applied running sts follow the line of the shoulder and do not pull over the shoulder from front to back, disturbing the drape of the fabric). The beads on the lozenges and half lozenges should be placed every 8th row so that they each lie in a depression formed by the moss (seed) st, and each line of beads should be separated by one row of vertical sts with the lines of beads alternating so that the beads on the following line lie at a level in the middle between the last beads.

The lines of beads on the small triangles should be placed in the same way as on the lozenges, but should be on every 4th row instead of every 8th row.

After attaching each bead take one long stitch on the WS, bringing the needle up in the correct position for the next bead, slide the next bead onto the yarn and take the needle through to the WS a short distance from where it came up. Cont in this way until all of the beads have been applied, taking care not to pull the yarn too tightly.

Sew Yoke to Back and Front across length of Yoke, then sew cast-on/cast- (bound-) off edges of Sleeves to vertical edge of armholes and sew cast- (bound-) off armhole shaping to sides of Sleeves.

Join side and sleeve seams. Press seams lightly on WS, following instructions on yarn label and omitting moss (seed) st and broken diagonal ribbing when pressing.

NIGHT OUT

ROWAN SILK AND WOOL

SIZES
To choose appropriate size see page 118
Finished measurement around bust 134[146:158]cm (54[58½: 63]")
Figures for larger sizes are given in brackets; where there is only one set of figures, it applies to all sizes.
See diagram for finished measurements of back, front and sleeves. To lengthen or shorten back and front, or sleeves see page 118.

MATERIALS
Rowan *Silk and Wool*
29[32:36] x 25g (1oz) balls in Coral (shade no. 855) *or* Black (shade no. 840) A
4 x 25g (1oz) balls in Oatmeal

(shade no. 854) B
One pair each 3¾mm (US size 5) and 4½mm (US size 7) needles *or size to obtain correct tension (gauge)*
Two stitch markers

TENSION (GAUGE)
21 sts and 27 rows to 10cm (4") over st st on 4½mm (US size 7) needles and using yarn double throughout
Check your tension (gauge) before beginning.

NOTES
The sweater can be worked in Coral or Black, but the yoke colour remains Oatmeal for both versions.
Use yarn double throughout.

When working with 2 colours in a row, do not carry yarn across back of work, but use a separate ball of yarn for each isolated area of colour, twisting yarns at back when changing colours to avoid holes.
On RS (knit) and WS (purl) rows of first 5 rows of chart, read chart from right to left to centre st, then skip centre st and read chart back to beg from left to right.
After neck has been divided and beg on 6th chart row, work left side of neck and shoulder first, reading chart from right to left on RS rows and from left to right on WS rows. When yarn is rejoined for right side of neck and shoulder, read chart from left to right on RS rows and from right to left on WS rows.

FRONT
Using smaller needles and using yarn B double, cast on 141[153: 165] sts.
1st rib row (RS) K1, *P1, K1, rep from * to end.
2nd rib row P1, *K1, P1, rep from * to end.
Change to yarn A (double) and cont to rep first and 2nd rib rows until ribbing measures 10cm (4") from beg, ending with a WS row.**
Change to larger needles and beg with a K row, work in st st until Front measures 46[50: 54]cm (18[19½:21]") from beg, ending with a RS row.
Beg with first chart row (P row), work in st st foll front neck chart (see *Notes* above for working from chart), beg as indicated for chosen size, until 5th chart row has been completed, so ending with a WS row.

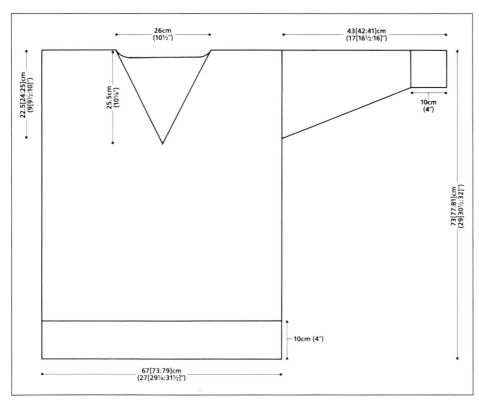

26cm (10½")   43[42:41]cm (17[16½:16]")
22.5[24:25]cm (9[9½:10]")
25.5cm (10¼")
10cm (4")
73[77:81]cm (29[30½:32]")
10cm (4")
67[73:79]cm (27[29¼:31½]")

Beautifully soft to touch, this yarn looks and feels wonderful. Slip this sweater on and you'll look a million.

'If you've got chests, this is the one. Truly elegant. I love it.'

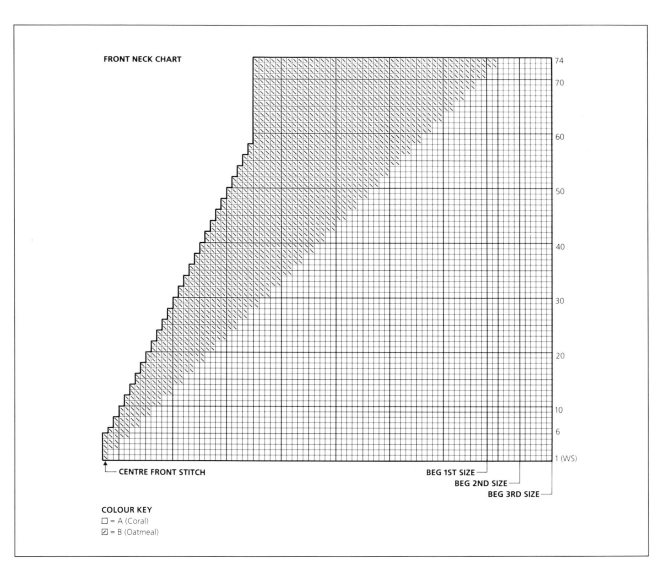

FRONT NECK CHART

74
70
60
50
40
30
20
10
6
1 (WS)

CENTRE FRONT STITCH

BEG 1ST SIZE
BEG 2ND SIZE
BEG 3RD SIZE

COLOUR KEY
□ = A (Coral)
☑ = B (Oatmeal)

Shape V-neck

Cont in st st throughout and foll chart, beg neck shaping on next row as foll:

Next row (RS) K first 70[76:82] sts in patt, turn leaving rem sts on a spare needle.

Working on first side of neck only and cont to foll chart for colour patt, dec one st at neck edge on next and every foll alt row until there are 43[49:55] sts, so ending with a WS row.

Cont foll chart and work 15 rows without shaping, so ending with a RS row.

Cast (bind) off in purl, foll colour patt for last row.

Return to rem sts and with RS facing, slip centre slip centre st onto a safety pin, rejoin yarn to rem sts and work in patt across row.

Complete 2nd side of neck as given for first side, reversing neck shaping.

BACK

Work as for Front to **.

Change to larger needles and beg with a K row, work in st st until Back measures 9cm (3½") less than Front to shoulder, ending with a WS row.

Next row (RS) K0[5:11]A, K0[1:1]B, *K1A, K1B, rep from * to last 1[5:11] sts, K1[5:11]A.

Next row P0[4:10]A, P141[145:145]B, P0[4:10]A.

Next row K0[5:11]A, K141[143:143]B, K0[5:11]A.

Rep last 2 rows until there are 9 rows less than Front to shoulder, ending with a WS row.

Shape Neck

Cont in st st throughout, beg neck shaping on next row as foll:

Next row (RS) K first 48[54:60] sts in patt as set, turn leaving rem sts on a spare needle.

Working on first side of neck only and cont in patt as set, dec one st at neck edge on next and every foll row 5 times in all, so ending with a WS row. 43[49:55] sts.

Work 3 rows without shaping.

Cast (bind) off as for Front.

Return to rem sts and with RS facing, rejoin yarn to rem sts and cast (bind) off centre 45 sts, then work in patt across row. Complete 2nd side of neck as given for first side, reversing neck shaping.

SLEEVES

Using smaller needles and yarn B double, cast on 46[48:50] sts. Work 2 rows in K1, P1 rib. Change to yarn A (double) and cont in rib until ribbing measures 10cm (4") from beg, ending with a WS row. Change to larger needles and beg with a K row, work in st st throughout *and at the same time* shape Sleeve by inc one st at each end next and every foll alt row 6[14:22] times in all, then inc one st at each end of every 3rd row 18[12:6] times. 94[100:106] sts. Work without shaping until Sleeve measures 43[42:41]cm (17[16½:16]") from beg, ending with a WS row. Cast (bind) off all sts. Make 2nd Sleeve in the same way.

NECKBAND

Press pieces lightly on WS, following instructions on yarn label and omitting ribbing. Join right shoulder seam. Using smaller needles and using yarn B double and with RS facing, pick up and K60 sts evenly down left front neck (this is approx 6 sts for every 7 row ends), slip st marker onto right-hand needle, K centre front st from the safety pin, slip st marker onto right-hand needle, pick up and K60 sts evenly up right front neck, 5 sts down right back neck, 45 sts across back neck, 5 sts up left back neck. 176 sts. Beg K1, P1 rib as foll:
1st row (WS) K1, (P1, K1) to centre front st, slip marker, P centre front st, slip marker, (K1, P1) to end.

2nd row Rib to 2 sts before centre front st, sl 1-K1-psso, slip marker, K centre st, slip marker, K2 tog, rib to end.
3rd row Rib to 2 sts before centre front st, K2 tog, slip marker, P centre st, slip marker, K2 tog, rib to end.
4th and 5th rows As 2nd and 3rd rows.
6th row As 2nd row.
Cast (bind) off in rib, removing st markers and working dec at either side of centre st as for 3rd rib row above while casting (binding) off the sts.

FINISHING

Using a single strand of yarn B, embroider spiral in chain stitch 1.5cm (½") below beg of chart on Front (see page 120).
Join left shoulder seam and neckband.
Place markers on Back and Front 22.5[24:25]cm (9[9½:10]") from shoulder seam.
Sew sleeves to Back and Front between markers.
Join side and sleeve seams.
Press seams lightly, following instructions on yarn label and omitting ribbing.

EVERYDAY CASUALS

We all need at least one sweater that we can put on anytime and feel relaxed and comfortable. Well, here are six to choose from. Whether it's a quiet *Vanilla Cable* or a loud *Garden Party*, you're sure to find a favourite in this collection.

NASHVILLE

R O W A N   D E N - M - N I T   C O T T O N

SIZES
To choose appropriate size see page 118
Finished measurement around bust 109[121:133:139]cm (43½[48½:53:55½]")
Figures for larger sizes are given in brackets; where there is only one set of figures, it applies to all sizes.
See diagram for finished measurements of back, front and sleeves after washing (see Note below about shrinkage after washing). To lengthen or shorten back and front, or sleeves see page 118.

MATERIALS
20[21:21:22] x 50g (1¾oz) balls of Rowan *Den-m-nit Indigo Dyed Cotton DK* in Nashville (shade no. 225)
One pair each 3¾mm (US size 5) and 4mm (US size 6) needles *or size to obtain correct tension (gauge)*
Six 2cm (¾") buttons

TENSION (GAUGE)
20 sts and 32 rows (after washing) to 10cm (4") over st st on 4mm (US size 6) needles
Check your tension (gauge) before beginning.

NOTES
When washed for the first time, this yarn will shrink in length by up to 20 per cent (one fifth); however, the width will stay the same (see page 122 for care and maintenance of Rowan Den-m-nit Indigo Dyed Cotton yarn before beginning). Follow knitting instructions carefully for knitted lengths.
Make a large tension (gauge) sample before beginning and wash and dry the sample before measuring.

DOUBLE MOSS STITCH
Worked over odd number of sts.
1st row K1, *P1, K1, rep from * to end.
2nd row P1, *K1, P1, rep from * to end.
3rd row As 2nd row.
4th row As first row.
These 4 rows are rep to form the patt.

LATTICE STITCH
Worked over a multiple of 6 sts plus one extra.
1st row (RS) K3, *P1, K5, rep from * to last 4 sts, P1, K3.
2nd row P2, *K1, P1, K1, P3, rep from * to last 5 sts, then work K1, P1, K1, P2.

3rd row K1, *P1, K3, P1, K1, rep from * to end.
4th row K1, *P5, K1, rep from * to end.
5th row As 3rd row.
6th row As 2nd row.
These 6 rows are rep to form the patt.

BACK
Using larger needles, cast on 41[53:65:71] sts.
1st row (RS) K into front and back of first st, *K1, P1, rep from * to end.
2nd row K into front and back of first st, K1, *P1, K1, rep from * to end.
3rd row K into front and back of first st, *P1, K1, rep from * to end.
4th row K into front and back of

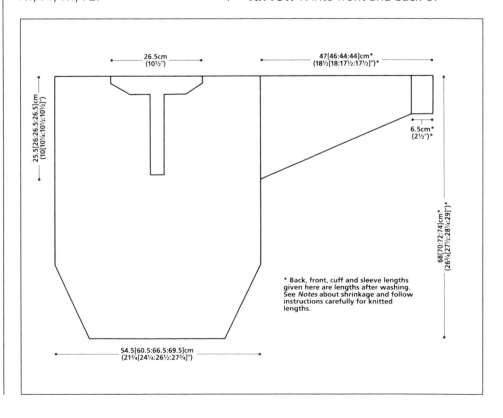

26.5cm (10½")

47[46:44:44]cm* (18½[18:17½:17½]")*

25.5[26.5:26.5:26.5]cm (10[10¼:10½:10½]")

6.5cm* (2½")*

68[70:72:74]cm* (26¾[27½:28¼:29]")*

54.5[60.5:66.5:69.5]cm (21¾[24¼:26½:27¾]")

* Back, front, cuff and sleeve lengths given here are lengths after washing. See *Notes* about shrinkage and follow instructions carefully for knitted lengths.

first st, P1, *K1, P1, rep from * to end.
Rep first-4th rows once more. 49[61:73:79] sts.
Next row (RS) K into front and back of first st, (K1, P1) 3 times, K to last 8 sts, (K1, P1) 4 times.
Cont in this way inc one st at beg of each row, working first 8 sts and last 8 sts of each row in moss (seed) st as set and working rem sts in st st, until there are 109[121:133:139] sts.
Cont to work first and last 8 sts in moss (seed) st and rem sts in st st, work without shaping until Back measures 51[53:55:57]cm (20¼[21:21¾:22½]") from beg, ending with a WS row.
Beg with first row of double moss st, work 5cm (2") in double moss, ending with a RS row.
Knit 3 rows, so ending with a WS row.**
Beg with first row of lattice st, work 20cm (7¾") in lattice st, ending with a RS row.
Knit 3 rows, so ending with a WS row.
Beg with first row of double moss st, work in double moss st until Back measures 86[88:90:92]cm 34[34¾:35½:36¼]" from beg, ending with a WS row.
Working in double moss st, cast (bind) off 28[34:40:43] sts at beg of next 2 rows.
53 sts rem. Cast (bind) off these 53 sts for back neck.

FRONT
Work as for Back to **.
Divide for neck opening and beg lattice st as foll:
Next row (RS) K3, (P1, K5) 7[8:9:10] times, P1, K3[3:3:0], turn leaving rem sts on a spare needle.
Working on first side of neck only, cont on these 49[55:61:64] sts in lattice st as set until there are same number of rows in lattice st as Back, ending with a RS row.
Knit 3 rows (garter stitch), so ending with a WS row.

Work in double moss st until Front measures 80[82:84:86]cm (31½[32¼:33:33¾]") from beg, ending with a RS row.
Shape Neck
Cont in double moss st and cast (bind) off 9 sts at beg of next row (neck edge). 40[46:52:55] sts.
Keeping to double moss st throughout and working on first side of neck only, dec one st at neck edge on every row 12 times. 28[34:40:43] sts.
Work without shaping until there are same number of rows as Back to shoulder.
Cast (bind) off in double moss st.
Return to rem sts and with RS facing, slip centre 11 sts onto a safety-pin, rejoin yarn to rem sts and work across row in lattice st, K3[3:3:0], P1, (K5, P1) 7[8:9:10] times, K3.
Complete 2nd side of neck to match first side, reversing all shaping.

SLEEVES
Using smaller needles, cast on 45[47:49:49] sts.
1st rib row K1, *P1, K1, rep from * to end.
2nd rib row P1, *K1, P1, rep from * to end.
Rep last 2 rows until ribbing measures 8cm (3") from beg, ending with a first row.
Next row (inc row) Rib 4[2:3:3], *work into front and back of next st – called inc 1 –, rib 1, inc 1 in next st, rib 2, rep from * 7[8:8:8] times more, rib 1[0:1:1]. 61[65:67:67] sts.
Change to larger needles and beg with first row of double moss st, work in double moss st and at the same time shape Sleeve by inc one st at each end of 3rd and every foll 4th row until there are 101[103:105:105] sts, keeping patt correct throughout.
Cont in double moss st without shaping until Sleeve measures 59[57:55:55]cm (23¼[22½:21¾:21¾]") from beg.

Cast (bind) off all sts in double moss st.
Make 2nd Sleeve in same way.

BUTTON BAND
Using smaller needles, cast on 11 sts.
1st rib row (RS) K1, *P1, K1, rep from * to end.
2nd rib row K2, P1, *K1, P1, rep from * to last 2 sts, K2.
Rep last 2 rows until band, slightly stretched, fits up neck opening from just below sts on safety-pin to beg of neck shaping.
Cast (bind) off in rib.
Sew Button Band to left-front vertical edge of neck opening.
Mark positions for 6 buttons on Button Band, the first 1.5 cm (½") from cast-on edge, the top one 1.5cm (½") below cast- (bound-) off edge, and the others evenly spaced between.

BUTTONHOLE BAND
Slip sts from safety-pin onto smaller needle so that RS is facing.
Work Buttonhole Band as for Button Band, making buttonholes to correspond with markers as foll:
1st buttonhole row (RS) Rib 4, cast (bind) off 3 sts, rib to end.
2nd buttonhole row Rib 4, cast on 3 sts, rib to end.

COLLAR
Using larger needles, cast on 8 sts.
1st row (RS) K5, *wrap yarn from front to back over top of right-hand needle to form extra loop on right-hand needle – called yo –, K1, yo, K2.
2nd row P6, *K into front and back of next st – called inc –, K3.
3rd row K4, P1, K2, yo, K1, yo, K3.
4th row P8, inc in next st, K4.
5th row K4, P2, K3, yo, K1, yo, K4.
6th row P10, inc in next st, K5.
7th row K4, P3, K4, yo, K1, yo,

This great yarn has all the properties of denim; the more you wash it the better it looks as it fades beautifully.

'Probably the most comfortable, easy-to-wear sweater you will ever own. Perfect for eating chocolate in, I found.'

ending with K5.

8th row P12, inc in next st, K6.

9th row K4, P4, *slip next 2 sts knitwise, one at a time, onto right-hand needle, insert tip of left-hand needle into fronts of*

slipped sts and K them tog – called slip, slip knit or ssk –, K7, K2 tog, K1.

10th row P10, inc in next st, K7.

11th row K4, P5, ssk, K5, K2 tog, K1.

12th row P8, inc in next st, K2, P1, K5.

13th row K4, P1, K1, P4, ssk, K3, K2 tog, K1.

14th row P6, inc in next st, K3, P1, K5.

15th row K4, P1, K1, P5, ssk, K1, K2 tog, K1.

16th row P4, inc in next st, K4, P1, K5.

17th row K4, P1, K1, P6, sl I-K2 tog-psso, K1.

18th row P2 tog, (K1, pass first st on right-hand needle over 2nd st and off needle) 5 times, P3, K4. (8 sts.)

Rep first-18th rows 7 times more to complete the Collar.

Cast (bind) off in knit.

FINISHING

Sew Buttonhole Band to right-front vertical edge of neck opening, then sew cast-on edge of Button Band to WS.

Press pieces lightly on WS with a warm iron over a damp cloth, omitting the ribbing and moss (seed) st.

Join shoulder seams.

Sew Collar to neck edge, leaving ribbed bands free.

Place markers on Back and Front 25.5[26:26.5:26.5]cm (10[10¼: 10½:10½]") from shoulder seam.

Sew sleeves to Back and Front between markers.

Join sleeve and side seams down to beg of curved shaping.

Wash and dry the sweater following the instructions on the yarn label.

Press seams lightly on WS with a warm iron over a damp cloth.

Sew on the six buttons.

DENIM PURL

ROWAN DEN-M-NIT COTTON

SIZES

To choose appropriate size see page 118

Finished measurement around bust 114[124:134:144]cm (45½[49½:53½:57½]")

Figures for larger sizes are given in brackets; where there is only one set of figures, it applies to all sizes.

See diagram for finished measurements of back, front and sleeves after washing (see Note *below about shrinkage after washing). To lengthen or shorten back and front, or sleeves see page 118.*

MATERIALS

20[21:22:23] x 50g (1¾oz) balls of Rowan *Den-m-nit Indigo Dyed Denim Cotton DK* in Nashville (shade no. 225)

One pair each 3¾mm (US size 5) and 4½mm (US size 7) needles *or size to obtain correct tension (gauge)*

TENSION (GAUGE)

20 sts and 36 rows (after washing) to 10cm (4") over patt on 4½mm (US size 7) needles *Check your tension (gauge) before beginning.*

NOTES

When washed for the first time, this yarn will shrink in length by up to 20 per cent (one fifth); however, the width will stay the same (see page 122 for care and maintenance of Rowan Den-m-

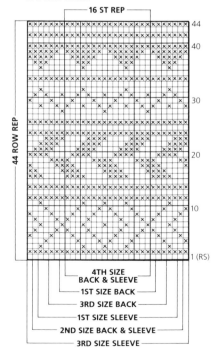

PATTERN CHART

16 ST REP

44 ROW REP

44
40
30
20
10
1 (RS)

4TH SIZE BACK & SLEEVE
1ST SIZE BACK
3RD SIZE BACK
1ST SIZE SLEEVE
2ND SIZE BACK & SLEEVE
3RD SIZE SLEEVE

STITCH KEY

□ = K on RS and P on WS
☒ = P on RS and K on WS

A simple but effective
stitch design gives this
sweater a lot of style and
because this lovely yarn
fades so well the stitch pattern gets to look better and
better.

*'Fab with jeans. You don't
have to be going to a
baseball match to wear it
either, honest.'*

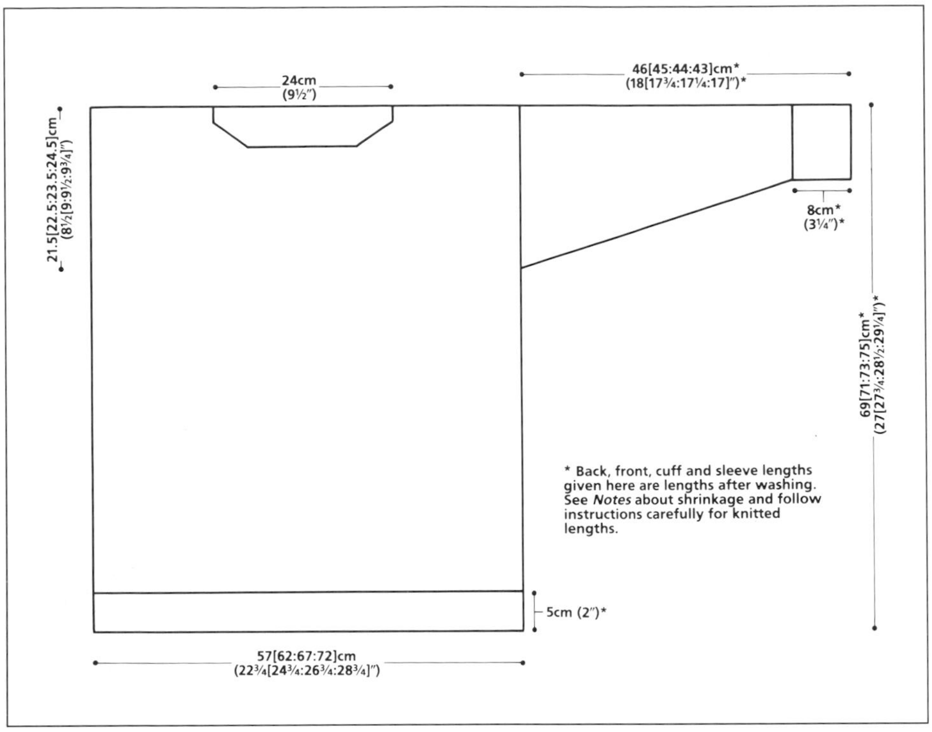
24cm
(9½")
46[45:44:43]cm*
(18[17¾:17¼:17]")*
21.5[22.5:23.5:24.5]cm
(8½[9:9½:9¾]")
8cm*
(3¼")*
69[71:73:75]cm*
(27[27¾:28½:29¼]")*
* Back, front, cuff and sleeve lengths given here are lengths after washing. See *Notes* about shrinkage and follow instructions carefully for knitted lengths.
5cm (2")*
57[62:67:72]cm
(22¾[24¾:26¾:28¾]")

nit Indigo Cotton *and denim yarns before beginning). Follow knitting instructions carefully for knitted lengths.*
Make a large tension (gauge) sample before beginning and wash and dry the sample before measuring.
Read chart from right to left for RS rows and from left to right for WS rows.

BACK
Using smaller needles, cast on 114[124:134:144] sts.
Work 24 rows in garter st (knit every row).
Change to larger needles and beg with first chart row (RS row), work in patt foll the chart as indicated for chosen size until all 44 rows have been worked.
Cont rep 44 chart rows until Back measures 87[89:91:93]cm (34¼[35:35¾:36½]") from beg, ending with a WS row.
Cast (bind) off 33[38:43:48] sts at beg of next 2 rows.
Slip rem 48 sts onto a st holder for back neck.

FRONT
Work as for Back until Front measures 81[83:85:87]cm (31¾[32½:33¼:34]") from beg, ending with a WS row.
Shape Neck
Next row (RS) Work 43[48:53:58] sts in patt, turn leaving rem sts on a spare needle.
Keeping patt correct throughout and working on first side of neck only, dec one st at neck edge on every row 10 times. 33[38:43:48] sts.
Work without shaping until there are same number of rows as Back to shoulder.
Cast (bind) off.
Return to rem sts and with RS facing, slip centre 28 sts onto a st holder, rejoin yarn to rem sts and work across row in patt.
Complete 2nd side of neck to match first side, reversing all shaping.

SLEEVES
Using smaller needles, cast on 42[44:46:48] sts.
Work 26 rows in K1, P1 rib.
Change to larger needles and beg with first chart row (RS row), work in patt foll the chart as indicated for chosen size until all of the 44 chart rows have been completed, then cont rep 44 chart rows *and at the same time* shape Sleeve by inc one st at each end of every 5th[5th:4th:4th] row until there are 86[90:94:98] sts, keeping patt correct throughout.
Cont in patt without shaping until Sleeve measures 57[56:55:54]cm (22½[22:21¾:21¼]") from beg.
Cast (bind) off all sts.
Make 2nd Sleeve in the same way.

NECKBAND
Press pieces lightly on WS with a warm iron over a damp cloth, omitting ribbing and garter st.
Join right shoulder seam.
Using smaller needles and with RS facing, pick up and K10 sts down left front neck, K28 from st holder, pick up and K10 sts up right front neck and K48 sts from back neck st holder. 96 sts.
Knit one row (WS).
Beg with 3rd chart row (RS row), work in patt foll the chart as indicated for *4th size back* until 14th row has been completed, so ending with a WS row.
Beg with a K row, work 12 rows in st st.
Cast (bind) off *loosely.*

FINISHING
Join left shoulder seam and neckband.
Place markers on Back and Front 21.5[22.5:23.5:24.5]cm (8½[9:9½:9¾]") from shoulder seam.
Sew Sleeves to Back and Front between markers.
Join side and sleeve seams.
Fold neckband in half to WS and sew in place.
Wash and dry pullover following instructions on yarn label.
Press seams lightly on WS with a warm iron over a damp cloth.

A bold cotton design with a
simple shape, why not try it
with a black background
and red and white shapes?
Either way it's so easy to
wear.

*'Want to be noticed? Don't
wear this if you're shy or if
you have no taste at all.'*

GEOMETRICS

R O W A N   H A N D K N I T   D K   C O T T O N

SIZE
One size only (see page 118 for
choosing size)
Finished measurement around
bust 158cm (63")
See diagram for finished
measurements of back, front and
sleeves. To lengthen or shorten
back and front, or sleeves see
page 118.

MATERIALS
Rowan *Handknit DK Cotton*
16 x 50g (1¾oz) balls in Ecru
(shade no. 251) A
7 x 50g (1¾oz) balls in Black
(shade no. 252) B
2 x 50g (1¾oz) balls in Cherry
(shade no. 298) C
One pair each 3¼mm (US size 3)
and 4mm (US size 6) needles *or
the size to obtain the correct*

tension (gauge)

TENSION (GAUGE)
20 sts and 28 rows to 10cm (4")
over st st on 4mm (US size 6)
needles
*Check your tension (gauge)
before beginning.*

NOTES
*Do not strand yarns across back
of work, but use a separate ball
yarn for each isolated block of
colour, twisting yarns at back
when changing colours to avoid
holes.*
*Read charts from right to left for
RS (knit) rows and from left to
right for WS (purl) rows; except
where charts need to be reversed
in which case read from left to
right for RS (knit) rows and from*

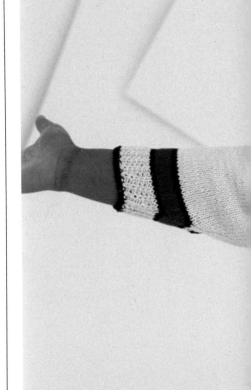

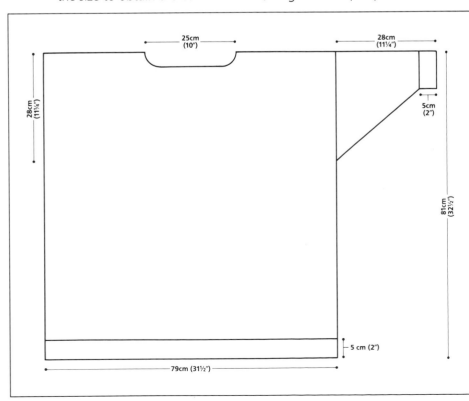

right *to left for WS (purl) rows as instructed.*

BACK

Using smaller needles and yarn B, cast on 158 sts.
Knit one row (WS).
Change to yarn A and beg K1, P1 twisted rib as foll:
1st rib row (RS) *K1 tbl, P1, rep from * to end.
Rep last row 11 times more. Do not break off yarn A, but leave at side of work.
Change to larger needles and using yarn B and beg with a K row, work 2 rows in st st. Do not break off yarn B.
Cont in st st throughout, work 6 rows in yarn C and 2 rows in yarn B. Break off yarns B and C.

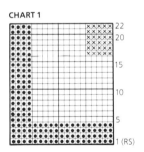

CHART 1

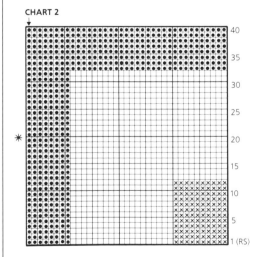

CHART 2

COLOUR KEY
□ = A (Ecru)
▣ = B (Black)
☒ = C (Cherry)

Work 6 rows in yarn A, so ending with a WS row.
Place position of chart 1 on next row as foll:
Next row (RS) K25A; then reading first chart row from right to left K19B; to complete row K114A.
Next row P114A; then reading 2nd chart row from left to right P19B; to complete row P25A.
The position of chart 1 is now set.
Cont in this way, working background in A and foll chart 1 for motif, until 6th chart row has been completed, so ending with a WS row.
Cont working each row of chart 1 as set *and at the same time* beg to work from chart 2 as foll:
Next row (RS) K25A, K19 sts of chart 1 as set, K43A; then reading first row of chart 2 from right to left K10C, K19A and K8B; K34A.
Next row P34A; then reading 2nd row of chart 2 from left to right P8B, P19A and P10C; P34A, P19 sts of chart 1 as set, P25A.
Cont in this way, working background in A and foll charts for motifs, until 22nd row of chart 1 has been completed, so ending with a WS row.
Next row (RS) K87A, K37 sts of chart 2 as set, K34A.
Cont in this way until 30th row of chart 2 has been completed, so ending with a WS row.
Next row (RS) K14C, K73A, K37 sts of chart 2 as set, K24A, K10C.
Next row P10C, P24A, P37 sts of chart 2 as set, P73A, P14C.
Cont in this way, working chart 2 in position as set and working 14 sts and 10 sts in yarn C in position as set, until 40th row of chart 2 has been completed, so ending with a WS row.
Next row (RS) K14C, K134A, K10C.
Next row P10C, P134A, P14C.
Rep last 2 rows twice more.
Work 8 rows in yarn A, so ending with a WS row.
Now *turn chart 2 on side so that*

asterisk is at lower edge of chart, and place position of chart 2 on next row as foll:
1st row (RS) K39A; then beg at *arrow* and reading first row of chart 2 from *left to right* to reverse motif K40B; K25A, K10C, K44A.
Next row P44A, P10C, P25A; then reading 2nd row of chart 2 from *right to left* P40B; P39A.
Cont in this way, working chart 2 in position as set and working 10 sts in yarn C in position as set, until 12th row of chart 2 has been completed, so ending with a WS row.
Next row (RS) K39A, K40 sts of chart 2 as set, K79A.
Next row P79A, P40 sts of chart 2 as set, P39A.
Cont working chart 2 as set *and at the same time* beg to work from chart 1 as foll:
Next row (RS) K39A, K40 sts of chart 2 as set, K46A; then reading first row of chart 1 from *left to right* to reverse motif K19B; K14A.
Next row P14A; then reading 2nd row of chart 1 from *right* to *left* P19B; P46A, P40 sts of chart 2, P39A.
Cont in this way until 22nd row of chart 1 has been completed, so ending with a WS row.
Next row (RS) K39A, K40 sts of chart 2 as set, K79A. This completes chart 2.
Work 5 rows in yarn A, 20 rows in yarn B and 4 rows in yarn A, so ending with a WS row.
Place position of chart 1 on next row as foll:
Next row (RS) K20A; then reading first row of chart 1 from right to left K19B; K119A.
Next row P119A; then reading 2nd row of chart 1 from left to right P19B; P20A.
Next row K20A, K19 sts of chart 1 as set, K96A; then reading first row of chart 1 from *left to right* to reverse motif K19B; K4A.
Next row P4A; then reading 2nd row of chart 1 from *right* to

left P19B; P96A, P19 sts of chart 1 as set, P20A.

Work 8 rows more as set, so ending with a WS row.

Next row (RS) K20A, K19 sts of chart 1 as set, K66A; then reading first row of chart 1 from right to left K19B; K11A, K19 sts of chart 1 as set, K4A.

Next row P4A, P19 sts of chart 1 as set, P11A; then reading 2nd row of chart 1 from left to right P19B; P66A, P19 sts of chart 1 as set, P20A.

Work 8 rows more as set, so ending with a WS row.

Next row K105A, K19 sts of chart 1 as set, K11A, K19 sts of chart 1 as set, K4A.

Work one row more as set.

Next row K105A, K19 sts of chart 1 as set, K34A.

Work one row more as set.

Next row (RS) K20A; then reading first row of chart 1 from *left* to *right* to reverse motif K19B; K66A, K19 sts of chart 1 as set, K34A.

Next row P34A, P19 sts of chart 1 as set, P66A; then reading 2nd row of chart 1 from *right* to *left* P19B; P20A.

Work 6 rows more as set, so ending with a WS row.

Next row (RS) K20A, K19 sts of chart 1 as set, K119A.

Work 5 rows more as set, so ending with a WS row.

Next row (RS) K20A, K19 sts of chart 1 as set, K78A; then reading first row of chart 1 from *left* to *right* to reverse motif K19B; K22A.

Next row P22A; then reading 2nd row of chart 1 from *right* to *left* P19B; P78A, P19 sts of chart 1 as set, P20A.

Work 6 rows more as set, so ending with a WS row.

Next row (RS) K117A, K19 sts of chart 1 as set, K22A.

Work 11 rows more as set, so ending with a WS row.

Shape Neck

Beg the neck shaping on the next row as foll:

Next row (RS) K60A, cast (bind) off centre 38 sts, work in patt as set to end.

Working on last set of sts only and working in yarn A only after next row is worked and motif is complete, dec one st at neck edge on next 4 rows, then dec one st on foll 2 alt rows. 54 sts. Work 3 rows without shaping. Cast (bind) off.

Return to rem sts and with WS facing, rejoin yarn A and complete to match other side, reversing all shaping.

FRONT

Work as for Back.

RIGHT SLEEVE

Using smaller needles and yarn B, cast on 50 sts.

Knit one row (WS).

Change to yarn A and work 12 rows in K1, P1 twisted rib as for

the ribbing on the Back.
Change to larger needles and beg with a K row, work in st st throughout inc one st at each end of next row and every foll alt row *and at the same time* work 2 rows in yarn B, 6 rows in yarn C, 2 rows in yarn B and 2 rows in yarn A, so ending with a WS row. 62 sts.**
Place position of chart 1 on next row as foll:
Next row (RS) Using yarn A, K into front and back of first st, K34A, then reading first row of chart 1 from right to left K19B, K7A, still using yarn A, K into front and back of last st. 64 sts.

Cont inc one st at each end of every alt row as set *and at the same time* foll chart 1 as set until 22nd chart row has been completed.
Work 2 rows in yarn A, so ending with a WS row. 86 sts.
Place position of chart 1 on next row as foll:
Next row (RS) Using yarn A, K into front and back of first st, K29A, then reading first row of chart 1 from *left* to *right* to reverse motif K19B, K36A, still using yarn A, K into front and back of last st.
Cont inc one st at each end of every alt row as set *and at the*

same time foll chart 1 as set until 22nd chart row has been completed, then work 3 rows in yarn A, so ending with a WS row. 112 sts.
Work 3 rows more in yarn A.
Cast (bind) off all sts.

LEFT SLEEVE
Work as for Right Sleeve to **.
Work in stripes of 12 rows in yarn A and (10 rows in yarn B, 10 rows in yarn A) twice *and at the same time* cont inc one st at each end of every alt row as set until there are 112 sts, ending with 3 rows without shaping after last inc row has been completed.
Cast (bind) off all sts.

NECKBAND
Press pieces lightly on WS with a warm iron over a damp cloth, omitting ribbing.
Join right shoulder seam.
Using smaller needles and yarn A and with RS facing, pick up and K12 sts down left front neck, 38 sts across centre front, 12 sts up right front neck, 12 sts down right back neck, 38 sts across centre back neck and 12 sts up left back neck. 124 sts.
Beg with a P row, work in st st in stripes of one row yarn A, 2 rows yarn B, 2 rows yarn A, 2 rows yarn C and 2 rows yarn A.
Using A only, knit 2 rows to form hemline, then beg with a K row, work 10 rows in st st.
Cast (bind) off loosely.

FINISHING
Join left shoulder seam and neckband.
Fold neckband in half to WS along hemline and sew in place.
Place markers on Back and Front 28cm (11¼") from the shoulder seam.
Sew Sleeves to Back and Front between markers.
Join side and sleeve seams.
Press seams lightly on WS with a warm iron over a damp cloth, omitting ribbing.

MUFFIN ZIGZAG

ROWAN HANDKNIT DK COTTON

SIZE

One size only (see page 118 for choosing size)
Finished measurement around bust 158cm (63")
See diagram for finished measurements of back, front and sleeves. To lengthen or shorten back and front, or sleeves see page 118.

MATERIALS

Rowan *Handknit DK Cotton*
17 x 50g (1¾oz) balls in Navy (shade no. 277) A
3 x 50g (1¾oz) balls in Muffin (shade no. 291) B
One pair each 3¼mm (US size 3) and 4mm (US size 6) needles *or size to obtain correct tension (gauge)*

TENSION (GAUGE)

20 sts and 28 rows to 10cm (4") over st st on 4mm (US size 6) needles
Check your tension (gauge) before beginning.

NOTES

When using 2 colours in a row, carry the yarn not in use loosely across back of work, weaving it around working yarn when necessary on chart 2.
Read charts from right to left for RS (knit) rows and from left to right for WS (purl) rows.

BACK

Using smaller needles and yarn B, cast on 157 sts.
Knit one row (WS).
Change to yarn A and beg K1, P1 twisted rib as foll:
1st rib row (RS) P1, *K1 tbl, P1, rep from * to end.
2nd rib row K1 tbl, *P1, K1 tbl, rep from * to end.

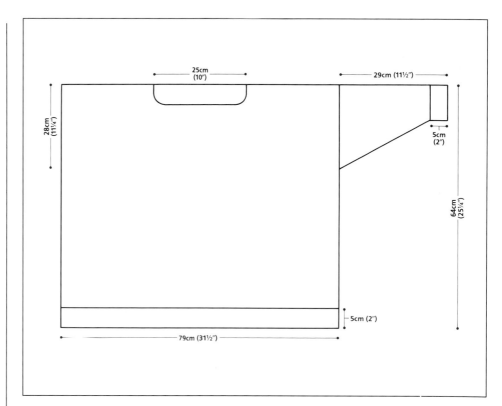

This sweater was specifically designed for Dawn and I'm very pleased to report that it has been a great success, everyone wants one; or so it seems when I'm ordering mountains of Navy and Muffin yarn.

'This was the first sweater Sylvie ever made for me and I wear it non-stop. That is a lie, I admit I do not wear it in the bath.'

CHART 1

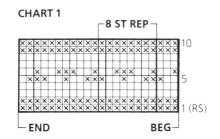

CHART 2

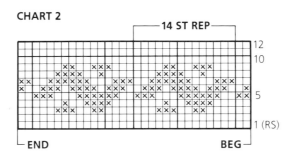

CHART 3

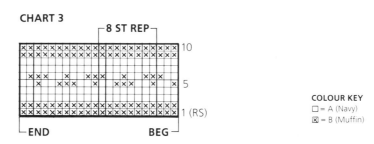

COLOUR KEY
☐ = A (Navy)
☒ = B (Muffin)

SLEEVE CHART

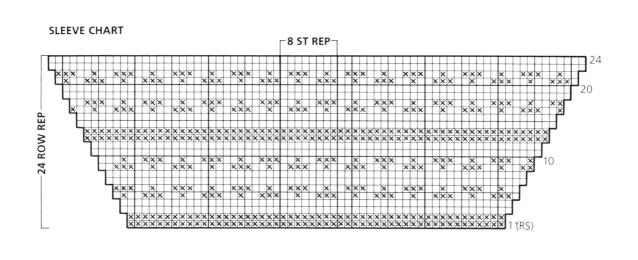

Rep last 2 rows 5 times more, inc one st at end of last row, so ending with a WS row. 158 sts. Change to larger needles and

beg with a K row, work 14 rows in st st, so ending with a WS row. Beg with first chart row (K row), work in st st foll chart 1 (see *Notes* above), beg and ending as indicated, until all 10 rows of chart have been completed, so ending with a WS row. Beg with first chart row (K row), work in st st foll chart 2, beg and ending as indicated on the chart, until all of the 12 rows of the chart have been completed, so ending with a WS row.

Beg with first chart row (K row), work in st st foll chart 3, beg and ending as indicated, until all 10 rows of chart have been completed, so ending with a WS row.**
Using A and beg with a K row, cont in st st until Back measures 60cm (23½") from beg, ending with a WS row.
Beg with first chart row (K row), work in st st foll chart 2 again until all 12 rows of chart have been completed, so ending with a WS row.
Cast (bind) off 54 sts at beg of next 2 rows.
Slip rem 50 sts onto a st holder for back neck.

FRONT
Work as for Back to **
Using yarn A and beg with a K row, cont in st st until Front measures 58cm (22¾") from beg, ending with a WS row.
(Chart 2 is not worked at top of Front.)
Shape Neck
Beg neck shaping on next row as foll:
Next row (RS) K60, turn leaving rem sts on a spare needle.
Working on first side of neck only and cont in st st, dec one st at neck edge on every row 4 times, then dec one st at neck edge on 2 foll alt rows. 54 sts.
Work without shaping until there are same number of rows as Back to shoulder.
Cast (bind) off.
Return to rem sts and with RS facing, slip centre 38 sts onto a st holder, rejoin yarn to rem sts and K across row.
Complete 2nd side of neck to match first side, reversing all shaping.

SLEEVES
Using smaller needles and yarn B, cast on 50 sts.
Knit one row (WS).
Change to yarn A and beg K1, P1 twisted rib as foll:

1st rib row (RS) *K1 tbl, P1, rep from * to end.
Rep last row until rib measures 5cm (2") from beg.
Change to larger needles and beg with a K row, work 2 rows in st st, so ending with a WS row.
Using yarn B, knit one row, inc one st each end. 52 sts.
Purl one row.
Beg with 3rd chart row (K row), work in st st foll sleeve chart until all 24 rows of chart have been completed *and at the same time* shape Sleeve by inc one st at each end of next and every foll alt row (as indicated on chart). 74 sts.
Cont to inc one st at each end of every alt row and keeping to chart patt as set throughout, work 38 rows more, so ending with a 14th chart row. 112 sts.
Change to A and work 2 rows more in st st.
Cast (bind) off all sts.
Make 2nd Sleeve in the same way.

COLLAR
Press pieces lightly on WS with a warm iron over a damp cloth, omitting ribbing.
Join right shoulder seam.
Using smaller needles and yarn A and with RS facing, pick up and K18 sts down left front neck, K38 sts from st holder, pick up and K18 sts up right front neck and K50 sts from back neck st holder. 124 sts.
Work 10cm (4") in K2, P2 rib working last row in yarn B.
Using yarn B, cast (bind) off in rib.

FINISHING
Join left shoulder seam and collar.
Place markers on Back and Front 28cm (11¼") from shoulder seam. Sew Sleeves to Back and Front between markers.
Join side and sleeve seams.
Press seams lightly on WS with a warm iron over a damp cloth.

VANILLA CABLE

ROWAN HANDKNIT DK COTTON

SIZES
To choose appropriate size see page 118
Finished measurement around bust 130[154]cm (51½[61½]")
Figures for larger size are given in brackets; where there is only one set of figures, it applies to both sizes.
See diagram for finished measurements of back, front and sleeves. To lengthen or shorten back and front, or sleeves see page 118.

MATERIALS
19[20] x 50g (1¾oz) balls of Rowan *Handknit DK Cotton* in Vanilla (shade no. 292)
One pair each 4mm (US size 6) and 4½mm (US size 7) needles *or size to obtain correct tension (gauge)*
Cable needle

TENSION (GAUGE)
19 sts and 26 rows to 10cm (4") over st st on 4½mm (US size 7) needles
Check your tension (gauge) before beginning.

BACK
Using smaller needles, cast on 122[146] sts.
Beg cable rib as foll:
1st rib row (RS) *P2, K4, rep from * to last 2 sts, P2.
2nd rib row *K2, P4, rep from * to last 2 sts, K2.
3rd rib row *P2, slip next 2 sts onto a cable needle and hold at back of work, K next 2 sts from left-hand needle, then K2 sts from cable needle, rep from * to last 2 sts, P2.
4th rib row As 2nd row.
Rep last 4 rows until cable rib measures 10cm (4") from beg,

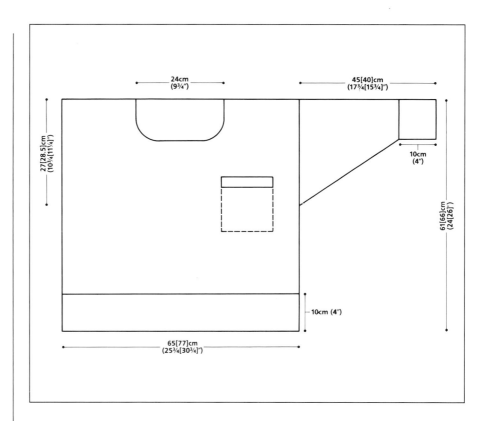

ending with a WS row.**
Change to larger needles and beg with a K row, work in st st until Back measures 61[66]cm (24[26]") from beg, ending with a WS row.
Cast (bind) off 38[50] sts at beg of next 2 rows.
Slip rem 46 sts onto a st holder for back neck.

FRONT
Before beg Front, make pocket lining.
Pocket Lining
Using larger needles, cast on 26 sts.
Work in st st until lining measures 12cm (4¾") from beg.
Break off yarn and slip sts onto a st holder to be used later.
Work Front as for Back to **.
Change to larger needles and beg with a K row, work in st st until Front measures 38[43]cm (15[17]") from beg, ending with a WS row.
Place Pocket
Cont in st st throughout, place pocket on next row as foll:
Next row (RS) K12[20] sts, slip next 26 sts onto a st holder, K the 26 sts of pocket lining from the st holder, K to end.
Work until Front measures 50[55]cm (19½[21½]") from beg, ending with a WS row.
Shape Neck
Beg neck shaping on next row as foll:
Next row (RS) K51[63], turn leaving rem sts on a spare needle.
Working on first side of neck only, cast (bind) off 2 sts at beg of next and every foll alt row 5 times in all, then dec one st at neck edge on 3 foll alt rows. 38[50] sts.
Work without shaping until there are same number of rows as Back to shoulder.
Cast (bind) off.
Return to rem sts and with RS facing, slip centre 20 sts onto a st holder, rejoin yarn to rem sts and K across row.
Complete 2nd side of neck to match first side, reversing all shaping.

SLEEVES
Using smaller needles, cast on 44[50] sts.
Work 10cm (4") in cable rib as for Back, ending with a WS row.
Change to larger needles and beg with a K row, work in st st, inc one st at each end of next and every foll alt row until there are 102[108] sts.
Cont in st st without shaping until Sleeve measures 45[40]cm (17¾[15¾]") from beg, ending with a WS row.
Cast (bind) off all sts.
Make 2nd Sleeve in the same way.

CABLE COLLAR
Press pieces lightly on WS with a warm iron over a damp cloth, omitting cable ribbing.
Join right shoulder seam.
Using smaller needles and with RS facing, pick up and K22 sts down left front neck, K20 sts from st holder, pick up and K22 sts up right front neck and K46 sts from back neck st holder. 110 sts.
Purl one row.
Work 10cm (4") in cable rib as for Back, ending with a WS row.
Cast (bind) off in P2, K4 rib.

FINISHING
Join left shoulder seam and collar.
Pocket Top
Using smaller needles and with RS facing, work first rib row across 26 sts of pocket top from st holder as foll:
1st rib row (RS) *P2, K1, K into front and back of next st, K1, rep from * to last st, P into front and back of last st. 32 sts.
Beg with a 2nd rib row, work 6 rows more in cable rib, so ending with a RS row.
Cast (bind) off in P4, K2 rib.
Sew pocket lining to WS of Front.
Sew ends of pocket top to RS.
Place markers on Back and Front 27[28.5]cm (10¾[11¼]") from shoulder seam.
Sew Sleeves to Back and Front between markers.
Join side and sleeve seams.
Press seams lightly on WS with a warm iron over a damp cloth, omitting cable ribbing.

Perfectly plain with a touch of detail, lovely in Vanilla but with Rowan's gorgeous cotton colour range why not try a soft sky blue or hot mango? The choice is yours.

'Classic, simple, gorgeous ... and so's the sweater ... if you don't like this one, you must be dead.'

Brighten up your day and everyone else's with this stunning trellis and floral design, knitted in softest designer double knit.

'If you don't want to wear it, you can eat it.'

GARDEN PARTY

R O W A N   D E S I G N E R   D K

SIZE
One size only (see page 118 for choosing size)
Finished measurement around bust 154cm (62")
See diagram for finished measurements of back, front and sleeves. To lengthen or shorten back and front, or sleeves see page 118.

MATERIALS
Rowan *Designer DK*
10 x 50g (1¾oz) balls in Hyacinth (shade no. 501) A
6 x 50g (1¾oz) balls in Cream (shade no. 1) B
2 x 50g (1¾oz) balls in Yellow (shade no. 13) C
2 x 50g (1¾oz) balls in Sea Green (shade no. 90) D
1 x 50g (1¾oz) ball in Red (shade no. 640) E
One pair each 3¾mm (US size 5) and 4½mm (US size 7) needles *or size to obtain correct tension (gauge)*

TENSION (GAUGE)
21½ sts and 29 rows to 10cm (4") over st st on 4½mm (US size 7) needles
Check your tension (gauge) before beginning.

NOTES
Do not strand yarn across back of work, but use a separate ball for each isolated area of colour, twisting yarns at back when changing colours to avoid holes. Read charts from right to left for RS (knit) rows and from left to right for WS (purl) rows.

BACK
Using smaller needles and yarn B, cast on 166 sts.
Beg moss (seed) st as foll:

1st row (RS) *K1, P1, rep from * to end.
2nd row *P1, K1, rep from * to end.
Rep last 2 rows to form moss (seed) st.
Work in moss (seed) st until Back measures 5cm (2") from beg, ending with a WS row.
Change to larger needles and beg with first chart row (K row), work in st st foll chart for back (see *Notes* above) and using yarn B for background until 50th chart row has been completed, so ending with a WS row.
Cont foll chart, but using yarn A for background until 132nd row has been completed, so ending with a WS row.

Shape Raglans
Cont to foll chart for colour patt throughout, cast (bind) off 13 sts at beg of next 2 rows. 140 sts.**
Dec one st at each end of next and every foll alt row 43 times in all. 54 sts.
Work one row without shaping.
Cast (bind) off.

FRONT
Work as for Back to **.
Dec one st at each end of next and every foll alt row 36 times in all. 68 sts.
Work one row without shaping, so ending with a WS row.
Shape Neck
Beg the neck shaping on the next row as foll:

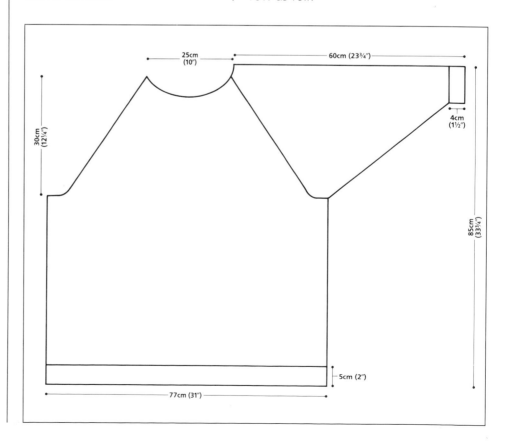

1 (RS) 10 20 30 40 50* 60 70 80 90 100

BACK AND FRONT CHART

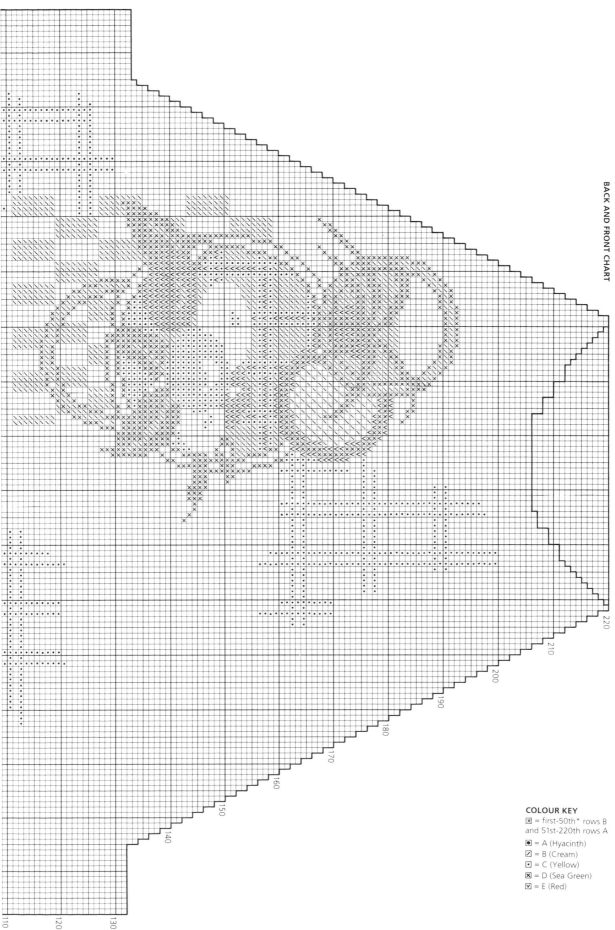

COLOUR KEY
⊠ = first-50th* rows B
and 51st-220th rows A

⊡ = A (Hyacinth)
☑ = B (Cream)
⊡ = C (Yellow)
⊠ = D (Sea Green)
☑ = E (Red)

BIG KNITS

115

SLEEVE CHART

COLOUR KEY
⊠ = first-44th* rows B
and 45th-162nd rows A

◉ = A (Hyacinth)
☑ = B (Cream)
⊡ = C (Yellow)
⊠ = D (Sea Green)
☑ = E (Red)

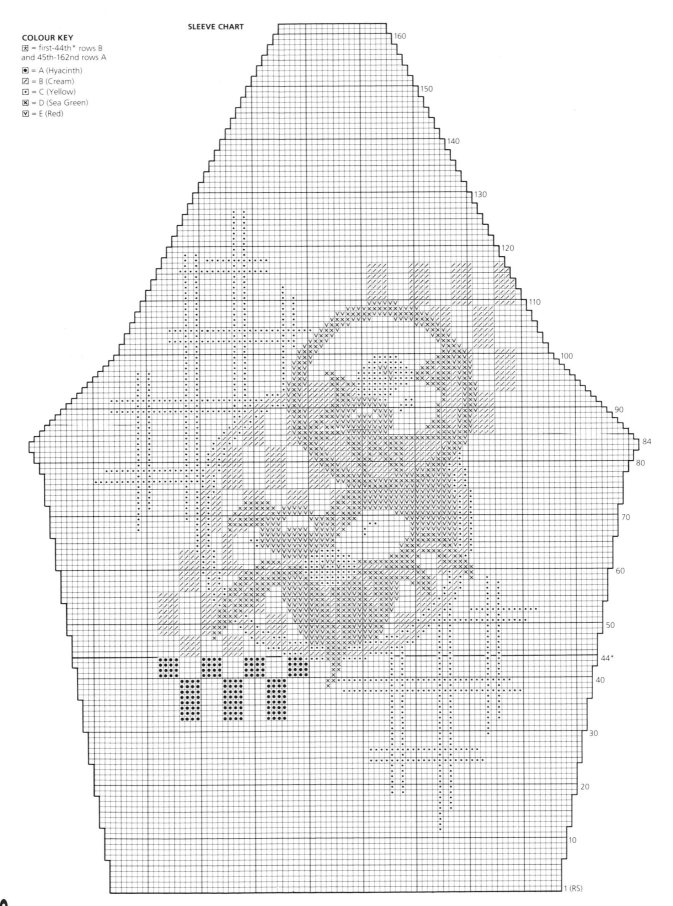

Next row (RS) Sl 1, K1, psso, K23, turn leaving rem sts on a spare needle.

Working on first side of neck only, shape neck by casting (binding) off 3 sts at beg of next and 2 foll alt rows, then dec one st at neck edge on every row *and at the same time* cont raglan shaping by dec one st at armhole edge on every alt row until 2 sts rem. Work 2 sts tog.

Fasten off rem st.

Return to rem sts and with RS facing, rejoin yarn and cast (bind) off centre 18 sts, K to last 2 sts, K2tog.

Work one row without shaping. Cont to shape neck by casting (binding) off 3 sts at beg of next and 2 foll alt rows, then dec one st at neck edge on every row *and at the same time* cont raglan shaping by dec one st at armhole edge on next and every foll alt row until 3 sts rem. Work 2 sts tog.

Cast (bind) off rem 2 sts.

SLEEVES

Using smaller needles and yarn A, cast on 67 sts.

Beg rib as foll:

1st rib row K1, *P1, K1, rep from * to end.

Break off yarn A and change to yarn B.

2nd rib row P1, *K1, P1, rep from * to end.

Last 2 rows form rib patt.

Work 11 more rows in rib, so ending with a first rib row.

Next row (inc row) P1, K into front and back of next st, *rib 3, K into front and back of next st, rep from * to last st, P1. 84 sts.

Change to larger needles and beg with a K row, work 6 rows in st st.

Inc one st at each end of next row. Work 4 rows more in st st without shaping.

Then beg with 12th chart row, work in st st foll sleeve chart and changing to yarn A for background on 45th row *and at the*

same time cont shaping Sleeve by inc one st at each end of every foll 6th row until there are 110 sts.

Cont to foll chart for colour patt throughout, inc one st at each end of foll 2 alt rows, so ending with a WS row. 114 sts.

Shape Raglans

Beg shaping raglans by dec one st at each end of every row 17 times in all. 80 sts.

Then work one row without shaping.

Dec one st at each end of next and every foll alt row 30 times in all. 20 sts.

Work one row without shaping. Cast (bind) off.

Make the 2nd Sleeve in the same way as the first.

COLLAR

Using smaller needles and yarn A, cast on 241 sts. Work 32 rows in K1, P1 rib as for cuffs, using yarn A throughout.

Cast (bind) off loosely in rib.

FINISHING

Press pieces lightly on WS with a warm iron over a damp cloth, omitting ribbing and moss (seed) st.

Join Sleeves to Front and Back at raglan edges. Join side and sleeve seams.

Beg and ending at centre of cast-(bound-) off sts of centre front neck, sew on collar, easing in fullness.

Press seams lightly on WS with a warm iron over a damp cloth.

KNITTING TECHNIQUES

HOW TO CHOOSE YOUR SIZE

Each design in this book is accompanied by a diagram giving the actual finished measurements. Using the diagrams you can choose which garment to knit depending on the desired looseness rather on a specific size that is supposed to 'fit' your particular measurements. Many of the designs are one size only, but where alternative sizes are given, you have a choice between a loose-fitting or a more close-fitting look.

Obviously, the greater the difference between the actual finished measurement and your bust measurement the looser the garment will be. If in doubt as to what type of fit you prefer, measure a favourite sweater to use as a guidline.

There is very little shaping on any of the designs in order that someone with a bust measurement of 92cm (36"), for example, can wear the same garment as someone with a 127cm (50") bust. The sweater would obviously look different on different wearers, but the style remains the same.

HOW TO ADJUST YOUR GARMENT

Although the garments included will fit a wide range of sizes, you may still wish to alter sleeve or body lengths, or even the body width in some instances.

Adjusting Sleeve Length

Sleeve length is a vital measurement and may be the only one needing adjustment if there are any adjustments at all to be made.

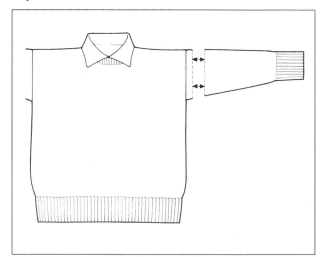

To make a sleeve longer (above), just work the extra rows *after* the sleeve shaping has been completed at the top of the sleeve. To shorten the length decrease the number of rows, making sure that the correct number of stitches has been increased first.

Most sleeve designs have a section which is worked straight (without shaping) at the top of the sleeve so that there is room for shortening. If,

however, you wish to shorten more than has been allowed for in the instructions you may have to work the increases closer together. For instance, if the pattern calls for increasing one stitch at each end of every 8th row, this may be altered to increasing at each end of every 6th row until the correct number of stitches has been increased.

Adjusting Body Length

The method for adjusting the body length of your garment depends on the specific design.

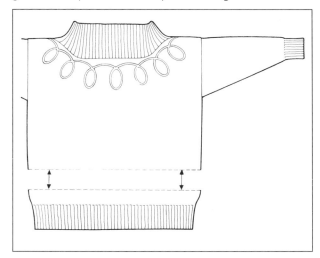

To alter length of a plain garment worked in a single colour (above), simply add or subtract the required number of centimetres (inches).

If the length is calculated by the number of rows instead of centimetres (inches) use the row tension (gauge) to work out the adjustment. For example, if you wish to lengthen by 5cm (2") and you are working to a tension (gauge) of 28 rows to 10cm (4") then add 14 rows. Always remember to make the body length alteration before the armhole shaping

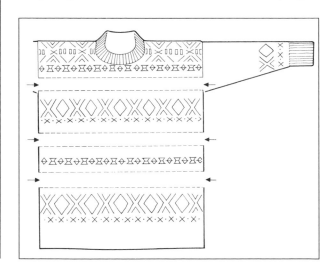

and before the neck shaping.

Changing lengths on a design which has a colourwork pattern must be done very carefully so as not to alter the charted motifs. Therefore, the alteration should be made either before the chart is begun or between the motifs. For instance, on *Winter Fairisle* (page 54) the gain or loss of rows should be evenly spaced between the fairisle patterns (see previous page).

Adjusting Body Width

To adjust the width of your garment, once you have decided how much you need to add or subtract, refer to the tension (gauge) to work out how many stitches this will involve. If, for example, you wish to remove 5cm (2") from the width of the back and front and the tension is 24 stitches to 10cm (4") then subtract 12 stitches.

The most important thing to remember is that after adding or subtracting stitches on a garment which later becomes shaped – the neck for instance – allow for the addition or subtraction of these stitches when following subsequent instructions.

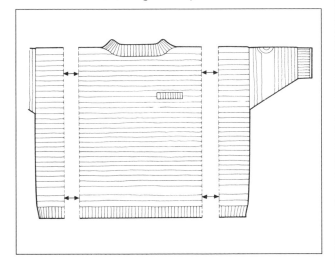

The loss or gain of stitches should be placed evenly on either side of the neck shaping so as not to alter the neck size (above). Also, remember that after changing the body width the sleeve length may need to be adjusted to compensate.

Again care must be taken when adjusting width on a design that follows a colourwork chart and it is not advised for an inexperienced knitter to attempt doing this.

TENSION (GAUGE)

The golden rule for knitters is – 'always check your tension'. Before starting any garment you should make a tension (gauge) sample in order to measure your tension (gauge) against that given in the pattern instructions. Failing to make a tension (gauge) sample may mean that the measurements of your finished garment will turn out to be very different from the measurements given in the instructions, thereby spoiling the appearance of the garment.

Make a tension (gauge) sample by using the yarn, needles and stitch pattern specified under 'Tension (Gauge)'. Knit the sample slightly larger than 10cm (4") square.

Smooth out the finished sample on a flat surface being careful not to stretch it. Using pins, mark out the number of stitches and rows given in the instructions for 10cm (4"). If the specified number of stitches knit up wider than 10cm (4"), then your knitting is too loose and you should change your needles to a smaller size. If they knit up narrower than 10cm (4"), then your knitting is too tight and you should change your needles to a larger size.

STRANDING YARN

One method used when knitting with more than one colour across a row is stranding the yarns on the wrong side of the knitted fabric.

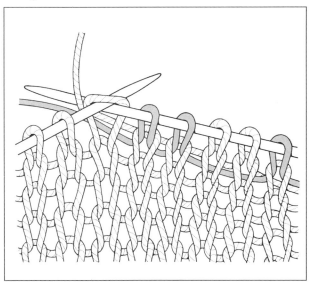

On a knit row, always keeping the contrasting colours at the back of the work, knit the required number of stitches with the first colour. Then drop the first colour and work with the 2nd colour as required, and so on.

The yarns should be stranded loosely across the back, but not so loosely that they form any suggestion of a loop. Strand in the same way on a purl row, always keeping the contrasting colours at the front of the work.

When using this method of colour knitting, strand yarn only over two to five stitches. If the yarn needs to be stranded over longer distances weave the yarn over and under the working yarn after every three or four stitches. Only use the stranding method if it is called for in the knitting instructions.

INTARSIA KNITTING
The other method used for colour knitting is called *intarsia*. In intarsia knitting the contrasting colours are only worked in isolated areas and are not stranded across the entire row. The knitting instructions will indicate when the motifs should be worked with separate balls of yarn in isolated areas.

When working in intarsia every time the colour is changed the yarns are twisted together to avoid creating a hole in the knitted fabric. A good example of this type of knitting is seen in the *Night Out* sweater (page 86), where it is obvious that it is not necessary to carry a particular colour past where it is needed in a row.

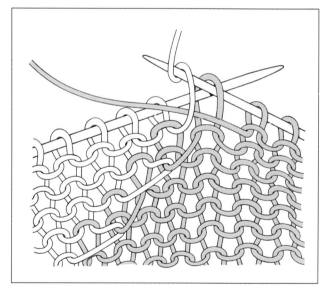

As with stranded knitting, the contrasting colours are always dropped to the wrong side of the knitting. The yarns are twisted together by crossing them before picking up the new colour (see above).

CHAIN STITCH EMBROIDERY
The spiral motif on the *Night Out* design (page 86) is worked in chain stitch on the front of the sweater after it has been knitted. The motif measures approximately 8cm (3") across and is worked from the middle of the spiral outwards.

Before beginning the embroidery mark the position of the centre of the spiral with a pin 6cm (2¼") below the point of the oatmeal yoke (above right), so that there will be a gap of about 1.5cm (½") between the finished spiral and the oatmeal yoke. Then place four pins 4cm (1½") from the centre to mark the diameter. If desired, you can baste the

spiral shape required onto the knitting.

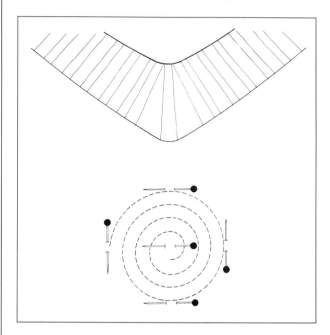

Once the position of the spiral has been marked, place the sweater on a flat surface.

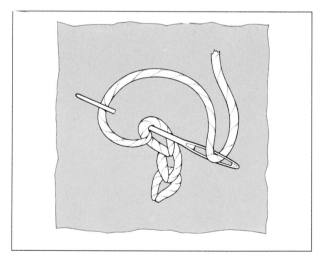

Using a blunt-pointed tapestry needle and the contrasting colour specified in the instructions, secure the yarn to the wrong side of the knitting and bring the needle through to the right side at the centre of the spiral. Holding the yarn with your thumb reinsert the needle where it last emerged and bring it out a short distance from where it entered (see above). Then pull the yarn through, keeping it under the needle. Continue in this way for the following stitches working outwards until the spiral has been completed, then fasten the yarn securely at the back.

BLANKET STITCH EMBROIDERY

A blanket-stitch edging is worked along the ribbing on the *Shells* sweater (page 10) after the garment has been completely sewn together.

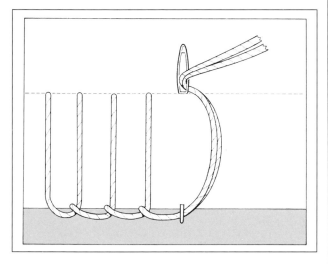

Using a blunt-pointed tapestry needle and two strands of the contrasting colour specified in the instructions, secure the yarn to the wrong side of the knitting and bring the needle through to the right side at the top of the ribbing at a side seam on the body. Insert the needle from right side to wrong side at the top of the ribbing a short distance to the right of where it first emerged, and through the cast-on stitches directly below back to the right side *in front* of the yarn (see above). Pull the yarn gently to form the first blanket stitch.

Continue in this way, spacing the stitches evenly along the knitting and ending at the lower edge. Fasten off the yarn on the wrong side. Work the blanket stitch edging along the cuffs and the neck in the same way.

FINISHING

Good finishing (described below) makes all the difference to the final success of your knitted garment.

Darning in Loose Ends

Loose ends on the wrong side of your knitting look untidy and if left loose are in danger of coming through to the right side and creating holes. While knitting when beginning a new yarn always leave long enough loose ends to finish off later.

To darn in loose ends after your garment pieces are completed, thread each end in turn into a blunt-pointed tapestry needle and weave it into the back of the knitting. The ends can then be safely trimmed close to the fabric. When working with different coloured yarns, darn the ends into the same coloured stitches for a neat effect.

Blocking and Pressing

Before pattern pieces are sewn together, they are usually blocked and pressed to ensure a good fit. It is always a best to check the yarn label for any special pressing instructions before beginning any blocking.

To prepare a padded surface for blocking lay a folded blanket on a table and cover it with a sheet. Place the knitted pieces wrong side up on top of the sheet, smoothing them out to the correct measurements. Being careful not to stretch or distort the fabric and making sure that all rows run in straight lines, pin the pieces in position using rustproof pins.

Then using a warm iron and a damp cloth, lay the iron gently on the fabric. Do not move the iron over the surface, but lift it up each time before moving it on. Remove the pins only after the knitting has cooled and dried completely. Do not press ribbing and use care when pressing raised patterns, such as the pattern on the *Travelling Vine* sweater (page 65).

Edge to Edge Seam

The edge to edge seam is useful when working with thicker knits, like the *Blue Days Jacket*, because it is almost invisible and forms no ridge thereby cutting down on unnecessary bulk. To work the seam place the pieces to be joined edge to edge, matching the pieces carefully row for row or, as on shoulders, stitch for stitch. Then, using the main colour, sew into the *head* of each stitch alternately.

Backstitch Seam

The backstitch seam is a strong, firm seam which is suitable for most garments but forms a ridge. Place the pieces to be joined together with right sides facing. Carefully match any colour patterns row for row or stitch for stitch. Work backstitch along the seam close to the edge, sewing into the centre of each stitch or row to correspond with the stitch or row on the oppostite piece.

CARE AND MAINTENANCE

All the yarns recommended for the designs in this book are made up of natural fibres – cotton, wool, silk and wool, or mohair and silk. With the exception of cotton these natural fibres should be treated with care and handwashed. Considering the work that has gone into knitting a garment, it would be extremely upsetting to ruin it by thoughtless aftercare.

Wool, Silk and Mohair

Although you should always refer to the yarn label for washing instructions for wool, silk and mohair yarns, as a general rule these fibres can be hand washed gently in lukewarm water using a mild detergent.

Never allow natural fibres to soak as this may result in colour loss and too much time in detergent will attack the fibres anyway. Do not lift the garment while wet as the weight of the water will till it out of shape. Instead, gently squeeze the water out before rinsing and rinse again until the water runs clear. If you have a short spin cycle on your washing machine, it is possible to spin the excess water out to reduce the drying time – but again use care. *Do not hang* the garment to dry, but instead dry it flat on a towel after you have laid it out and smoothed it gently into shape.

If washing has flattened your mohair knitting, the fibres can be teased to fluff them out by using a soft bristle brush and very light strokes so as not to pull out the stitches.

Cotton and Cotton Den-m-nit

Again, for cotton yarns refer to the yarn label for care instructions, especially for Rowan *Den-m-nit Indigo Dyed Cotton.* Cotton does not have to be treated with quite as much caution as wool and therefore it is possible to wash cottons in the washing machine on a gentle cycle. The addition of fabric conditioner when washing cotton will keep it soft to the touch.

Rowan *Den-m-nit Indigo Dyed Cotton* possesses the same unique features as denim jeans. It will shrink and fade as it is worn and washed. The dye loss will be the greatest during the initial wash. The appearance of the garment will, however, be greatly enhanced with additional washing. It should be washed in the washing machine using fabric conditioner and tumble dried.

Please note that when knitting with this type of denim yarn the dye occasionally comes off onto the knitters hands. The colouring is removed easily but may 'smudge' onto other fabrics it comes into contact with before it has been washed and dried the first time.

KNITTING ABBREVIATIONS

alt	alternate(ly)
approx	approximately
beg	begin(ning)
cm	centimetre(s)
cont	continu(e)(ing)
dec	decreas(e)(ing)
foll	follow(s)(ing)
g	gramme(s)
inc	increas(e)(ing)
K	knit
m	metre(s)
mm	millimetre(s)
oz	ounce(s)
P	purl
patt	pattern
psso	pass slip stitch over
rem	remain(s)(ing)
rep	repeat(ed)(ing)
RS	right side(s)
sl	slip
st(s)	stitch(es)
st st	stocking (stockinette) stitch
tbl	through back of loop(s)
tog	together
WS	wrong side(s)
yd	yard(s)

ACCESSORIES

Shells (pages 8, 11 and 12) Fish earrings by Alex Monroe from *The Outlaws Club*.

Gone Fishing (pages 8 and 18) Trousers from *Forgotten Woman*, fishbone earrings from *The Outlaws Club*, hat from *The Hat Shop*.

Shells, Gone Fishing and Japanese Fish (pages 20 and 21) Dawn: Fishbone earrings from *The Outlaws Club*. Sharon: Jogging pants from *Dickens & Jones*, hat from *The Hat Shop*. Jane: Trousers from *Forgotten Woman*, earrings by *Adrien Mann*, hat from *The Hat Shop*.

Japanese Fish (pages 22 and 23) Jogging pants from *Dickens & Jones*, hat from *The Hat Shop*, fish earrings by Alex Monroe from *The Outlaws Club*.

Nautical (pages 28 and 29) Jogging pants from *The Base*, earrings by *Adrien Mann*.

Chilli Cardigan, Skirt and Sweater (pages 33 and 34) Sharon: Skirt from *The Base*, jewellery by *Butler & Wilson*. Jane: Blouse from *Selfridges*, jewellery by *Butler & Wilson*.

Paisley Shawl (pages 38 and 39) Earrings from *The Outlaws Club*.

Border Jacket and Skirt (pages 41 and 43) Jewellery by *Adrien Mann*.

Floral Cardigan (pages 30, 49 and 50) Cotton jersey skirt from *Selfridges*, t-shirt from *The Base*, earrings from *The Outlaws Club*.

Winter Fairisle (pages 55 and 59) Cotton jersey skirt from *Forgotten Woman*, jewellery from *The Outlaws Club*.

Firefly, Nelson and Nautilus (pages 61, 62 and 63) Jane: Jogging pants from *The Base*, earrings by *Adrien Mann*. Dawn: Skirt from *Dickens & Jones*, earrings by *Adrien Mann*. Sharon: Jogging pants from *Forgotten Woman*, earrings by *Adrien Mann*.

Travelling Vine (pages 64 and 67) Wool jersey skirt from *Xtra*, hat from *The Hat Shop*, earrings from *The Outlaws Club*.

Moss Stitch Blazer (pages 52, 69 and 70) Dawn: T-shirt from *Selfridges*, earrings from *The Outlaws Club*. Jane: T-shirt from *Xtra*, earrings from *The Outlaws Club*.

Blue Days jacket (pages 72 and 75) Skirt from *Selfridges*, blouse from *Dickens & Jones*, earrings from *The Outlaws Club*.

Night Out (pages 76, 87 and 89) Dawn: Linen trousers from *The Base*, earrings from *The Outlaws Club*. Sharon: Velvet trousers from *Forgotten Woman*, hat from *The Hat Shop*, jewellery by *Butler & Wilson*.

ACKNOWLEDGEMENTS

We would like to say many thanks to everyone involved in this book.

To Kathleen Hargreaves at Rowan, Anne Farmer and her wonderful Cambridgeshire Knitters, Betty Kennedy and Mrs Cowood for their lovely work as usual.

Trevor Leighton for the great photographs and the jokes! Susie Slack the stylist, Keith Harris and Charlie Duffy for hair and make-up. Adrian Sanders — Trevor's assistant — a very important person as he had to get the chocolate for our glamorous models Sharon Henry and Jane Crossley.

Finally, a very big thank you to Valerie Buckingham at Century for her help and support, Sally Harding who is probably the most efficient person in the Western hemisphere and Heather Johns for her superb design of the book. Also Marilyn Wilson and Dennis Hawkins for pattern checking and charts and diagrams.

Soft Focus (pages 78 and 80) Pleated skirt from *Xtra*, earrings by *Butler & Wilson*.

Evening pearls (pages 83 and 85) Earrings from *The Outlaws Club*.

Nashville and Denim Purl (pages 92, 95-97 and 99) Hat from *The Hat Shop*, jewellery from *The Outlaws Club*.

Geometrics (pages 101, 103 and 104) Skirt from *Forgotten Woman*, earrings from *The Outlaws Club*.

Muffin Zigzag (pages 105, 106 and 108) Trousers from *Forgotten Woman*, earrings by *Adrien Mann*.

Vanilla Cable (pages 109 and 111) Linen trousers from *The Base*, hat from *The Hat Shop*, jewellery from *The Outlaws Club*.

Garden Party (pages 90, 112 and 117) Jogging pants from *Forgotten Woman*, earrings from *The Outlaws Club*.

Adrien Mann available from most major stores in UK.
The Base, 55 Monmouth Street, London WC2.
Butler & Wilson, 20 South Molton Street, London W1 and branches.
Dickins & Jones, Regent Street, London W1.
Forgotten Woman, 20 Marylebone High Street, London W1.
The Hat Shop, 9 Gees Court, St Christophers Place, London W1.
The Outlaws Club, 49 Endell Street, London WC2.
Selfridges, Oxford Street, London W1.
Xtra, 115 Golders Green Road, London NW11.

YARN INFORMATION

Whenever possible it is best to use the yarn specified in the knitting pattern instructions. Contact Rowan Yarns (addresses on next page) for information on your nearest stockist. When ordering a specific yarn, specify the colour by the shade number rather than the colour name.

If you wish to purchase a substitute yarn, choose a yarn of the same type and the same weight as the recommended yarn. The descriptions (below) of the various Rowan yarn types should be used as a guide to yarn weight and type (i.e., mohair, cotton, wool, et cetera). When purchasing a substitute yarn, calculate the amount needed by the number of metres (yards) required rather than by the number of grammes (ounces).

Rowan *Botany* (100% pure new wool)
approx 115m (125yd) per 25g (1oz) hank

Rowan *Bright Tweed* (100% pure new wool)
approx 100m (109yd) per 100g (3½oz) hank

Rowan *Chunky Tweed* (100% pure new wool)
approx 100m (109yd) per 100g (3½oz) hank
(interchangeable with *Bright Tweed*)

Rowan *Den-m-nit Indigo Dyed Cotton DK* (100% cotton)
approx 93m (102yd) per 50g (1¾oz) ball

Rowan *Designer DK* (100% pure new wool)
approx 115m (125yd) per 50g (1¾oz) ball

Rowan *Handknit DK Cotton* (100% cotton)
approx 82m (90yd) per 50g (1¾oz) ball

Rowan *Kid/Silk* (70% kid mohair and 30% mulberry silk)
approx 62m (67yd) per 25g (1oz) ball

Rowan *Lightweight DK* (100% pure new wool)
approx 67m (73yd) per 25g (1oz) hank

Rowan *Magpie Aran* (100% pure new wool)
approx 150m (164yd) per 100g (3½oz) hank

Rowan *Rowanfleck DK* (85% wool and 15% cotton)
approx 120m (131yd) per 50g (1¾oz) ball

Rowan *Rowanspun Tweed* (100% pure new wool)
approx 170m (186yd) per 100g (3½oz) hank

Rowan *Silk and Wool* (50% mulberry silk and 50% superfine botany wool)
approx 93m (102yd) per 25g (1oz) ball

Rowan *Silkstones* (58% silk and 48% wool)
approx 200m (218yd) per 50g (1¾oz) ball

ROWAN YARNS

Rowan yarns are widely available in yarn shops. For further information on stockists and mail order sources contact the following:

UK: Rowan Yarns, Green Lane Mill, Holmfirth, West Yorkshire HD7 1RW, England. Tel: (0484) 681881

AUSTRALIA: Sunspun Enterprises Pty Ltd, 191 Canterbury Road, Canterbury, Victoria 3126. Tel: (03) 830 1609

BELGIUM: Susan Higgin, Ma Campagne, rue du Village 4, Septon 5482, Durbuy. Tel: 086 213451

CANADA: Estelle Designs and Sales Ltd, 38 Continental Place, Scarborough, Ontario M1R 2T4. Tel: (416) 298 9922

CYPRUS: Litsa Christofides, Colourworks, 12 Parnithos St, Nicosia. Tel: 047 2933

DENMARK: Mosekonens Vaerksted, Mosevej 13, L1 Binderup, 9600 Aars. Tel: 45 8 656065

FINLAND: Stockmann, P.O. Box 220, SF-00101 Helsinki. Tel: 01 12151

HOLLAND: Henk & Henrietta Beukers, Dorpsstraat 9, 5327 AR Hurwenen. Tel: 31 4182 1764

ITALY: La Campagnia Del Cotone, Via Mazzini 44, 10123 Torino. Tel: 011 878381

JAPAN: DiaKeito Co Ltd, 1-5-23 Nakatsu, Oyodo-Ku, Osaka 531. Tel: 06 371 5653

NEW ZEALAND: Creative Fashion Centre, PO Box 45083, Epuni Railway, Lower Hutt. Tel: (04) 674 085

NORWAY: Eureka, P.O. Box 357, 1401 Ski. Tel: 0987 1909

SINGAPORE: Classical Hobby House, 1 Jin Anak Bukit, No. B2-15 Bukit Timah Plaza. Tel: 466 2179

SWEDEN: Wincent, Luntmakargtan 56, 113 58 Stockholm.

WEST GERMANY: Textilwerkstatt, Friedenstrasse 5, 3000 Hanover 1. Tel: (0511) 818001

USA: The Westminster Trading Corporation, 5 Northern Boulevard, Amherst, NH 03031. Tel: (603) 886 5041

PEARL BEADS

5mm pearl beads (P5 in Ivory) for the *Evening Pearls* sweater are available mail order from Ells & Farrier Ltd, 20 Princes Street, Hanover Square W1, London, England (Tel: 01-629 9964).

INDEX